ALSO BY BRIAN SACK

In the Event of My Untimely Demise

The B.*** S.__ __ of A.

A Primer in Politics for the Incredibly Disenchanted

BRIAN SACK

THRESHOLD EDITIONS

NEW YORK   LONDON   TORONTO   SYDNEY

CONTENTS

Part the Third: Washington, B.S.
Wherein we enter the bowels of the nation's capital looking for "It" and investigate how "It" permeates everything

Part the Fourth: Knee Deep and Shovel Ready:
Wherein, finding ourselves standing in "It,"
we explore ways to get out of "It"

PREFACE

Wherein "It" is defined

𝕿𝖍𝖊 "It" that will be repeatedly referred to in this book should be understood to be the "bullshit of America" as the title of the book suggests.

Also, it should be noted that this is a humor book.

I'm hoping that fact will become obvious—or in fact was already obvious after you took a quick glance at the cover—but I feel the need to remind you:

This is a humor book.

I felt like I had to say this just in case you get mad.

Now, why would you get mad? Well, the book's subject is politics and as we've seen quite often—such as every single time someone talks politics with friends or strangers, in person or on the Internet—people seem more and more inclined to get mad. Teeth-gritting, hateful-thing-saying, muttering and cursing mad. Especially in these really, really disenchanting and partisan times. Case in point: I was recently at a very nice dinner where someone called someone else an "idiot" because of who they voted for in 2008. This was inaccurate, as the accused "idiot" speaks four languages and actually finished college whereas the accuser doesn't and didn't.

Why people are so easily able to attain these stratospheric levels of anger isn't rocket science. Folks are used to staying well inside their comfort zones. They read the books and weblogs that reinforce their views, tune in to the TV and radio shows that tell them what they want to hear and generally shy away from encounters with viewpoints or facts they don't know how to handle or want to consider. As a result, in the event they stumble across one of the myriad differing opinions that do exist in the world, they're taken outside their comfort zone. When that happens, even for a moment, they get disoriented, bothered, mad. If you've spent any time on a comment thread anywhere in the vast reaches of cyberspace you know what I'm saying is true.

Now, since I've actually made an effort to be nonpartisan in my book (no, really!), I run the risk of making someone from anywhere on the political spectrum angry about *something*. There's really no getting around it if you're going to observe something objectively—to be *fair and balanced,* as they say. Presumably with tongue firmly planted in cheek.

The only way to avoid making someone mad would be to embrace partisanship and do what everyone else does: Write a book like *Liberals Are Pinko Commies* or *The GOP Is Hitler.* In doing so I'd join a long line of authors who have large, enthusiastic, built-in, partisan readerships. Because, let's face it, the only people who would buy a book like *Liberals Are Pinko Commies* would be people who believe liberals are in fact pinko commies. And maybe the one guy from the *New York Times* book review who picked up a copy in order to write a negative review. Likewise, the only people walking around with a copy of *The GOP Is Hitler* would be the folks who already believe the GOP is comparable to the deranged leader of the Nazis who was a great orator but unfortunately started a global war and in the course of trying to murder an entire ethnicity caused millions of deaths.

So yes, the easiest thing for me to do would be to write something solely for people who agreed on every single thing I was writing. Heck, a lot of them might not even open the book—they'd just add it to their collection of unread, partisan books so that everyone who enters their house can look around and ascertain where they stand politically. I'd probably sell more books that way. They'd be happy. I'd be happy. Everyone would be happy.

But not really. Because that kind of silly partisanship begets even more partisanship. And partisanship is one of many things screwing the country up at the moment, as you may have noticed. It's unhealthy. It's awkward. It can get really ugly. When someone is rabidly partisan they will defend anything their party does no matter how ludicrous, stupid or reprehensible. Take voter fraud, for example. When one side screams about voter fraud and the other side shrugs it off because they benefited from it, they might score a temporary win but it's ultimately bad for everyone. Bad for you, for me, for a democracy in general. When the only goal is victory over your political adversaries at all costs, you tend to cut corners and sacrifice things like common sense, morality and principle. Those are really things you should hold on to as hard as you can because their absence tends to come back and bite you on the bum-side.

We're living in a time when people are quite incredibly disenchanted with politics. Credibly so. Not just the other guy's politics, but politics as a whole. The kind of politics that asks you to support and defend candidates who have no business running for office. The kind of politics that has you cheerleading a very bad idea solely because it makes the other guys insanely mad. The kind of politics that has one party fighting another party tooth and nail solely to keep anything from being accomplished. The kind of politics where our public servants have become our masters—telling us how we're going to live, spending our money like a spoiled-rotten, spendthrift teenager and using political office for personal enrichment as it was never intended. The kind of politics that's not just bad for the business of governance but that also threatens the country unlike any insane, saber-wielding Middle Eastern theocrat or half-literate Latin American dictator ever could.

We spend a lot of time scanning the horizon (and groping our travelers) looking for threats, but we're often blind to threats that actually exist. These are threats that aren't going to be coming from overseas because they are from right here. If we're going to fall apart anytime soon it's going to be from the inside. You know, in the midst of a hyperpartisan, anything-goes, ends-justifies-the-means atmosphere where people are so eager to "beat" the other guys that they forget the things that made this country one of the better places on earth to find oneself. Sure, the sunsets are nice but it's the liberty and security and prosperity that we enjoy that has prompted people to drag themselves here for as long as they have. I like the place.

So, I wrote this book. I did so partly to lighten the atmosphere—like a kid who runs between bickering parents and makes a funny face in an effort to get them to stop. And partly to point some fingers in an objective manner in the hopes that folks might stop all the bickering for a moment and go, "Yeah, you're kind of right."

It felt like a good time to be a uniter—not a divider. And not a uniter like George W. Bush wanted to be, because he was actually one of the most divisive presidents in history. No, a uniter in the sense that I'd be able to stand back with my fellow countrymen and call bullshit on everyone and everything in politics that deserved to have bullshit called on it—regardless of his, her or its political affiliation.

Back to what "It" is: That was the genesis of *The B.S. of A.*

Now, I suppose a book of a political nature should offer the reader details of the political background of the person writing it. After all, partisanship breeds suspicion. If you're at all inclined to partisanship, the natural assumption is that someone saying something you might not totally agree with must have some kind of agenda. Conspiracies abound at every corner! Everyone is suspect! Certainly, many of you are thinking, the author must be writing this book *for a reason.*

So, yes. Truth be told, I am writing this book because I like to write. And I like politics. And I like to entertain. And if there's one topic in dire need of some damned levity—it's politics. Today's politics has people seething, barking, foaming at the mouth, saying/writing/tweeting/posting horrible things to one another. Levity is needed, *stat,* lest another otherwise enjoyable dinner be rendered uncomfortable by someone saying "You're an idiot" to someone else at the table.

Do I have a political agenda? No. I'm certainly not looking to advance any party. I don't have any particular candidates that I'm rooting for. I like to follow and talk politics—in a civil manner, using my indoor voice, and rarely with strangers. Like most people I think the government is broken and I'd like it to be fixed sometime in the near future. I have my own ideas about how people might go about doing that, were they so inclined. Some of those ideas are probably good. Some are probably unrealistic. Others might be simplistic. I think it's important to detach emotionally from issues and evaluate them objectively—like a Vulcan with normal ears and eyebrows. I'm not afraid to entertain alternate viewpoints and I'm not afraid to change my mind if, once entertained, those viewpoints wind up making more sense. There are also issues that I am unwilling to form strong opinions on because I just don't know enough about them. I often wish a lot more people felt the same way.

I grew up in an average, fairly apolitical household. There was no ranting or raving about politics going on at dinner. A glance at the bookshelf didn't offer any insight into the political leanings of the occupants, just lots of history books and an encyclopedia so outdated it mentioned that NASA hoped to one day land on the moon. There was nothing hanging on the walls that would help either. No bumper stickers on the cars offering clues. No campaign signs on the lawn before elections. Nothing. My parents never made us wear political candidate T-shirts and never took us to rallies to make us carry signs for things we knew nothing about. I'm grateful for that. Prior to the 2008 election I was profoundly creeped out by all the kids at the playground wearing Obama shirts, just as I would have been had they been wearing McCain shirts. Or Reagan shirts. Or Clinton skirts. They're kids! Keep them out of it.

My parents were Independents who favored whatever party had the best candidate. They liked John Kennedy, but Ted Kennedy turned them off completely. At the request of a friend, they hosted a fund-raiser for Democratic representative Gerry Studds back in the day, and declined holding another one after he was caught in a sex scandal.

I can't speak for grandpa Sam, who died in my late teens, but my paternal grandmother, Bertha, was a wonderful, adorable woman loved by everyone who knew her. This contrasted dramatically with her (hilarious) deep-seated hatred for Mike Dukakis, whom she routinely dismissed as "Mike Do-Caca." She also did not hesitate to tell everyone that she lived in "Taxachusetts." She loved Richard Nixon. There was absolutely nothing you could have said or done to convince her that Richard Nixon was anything but a saint. Nothing. Not the crookery, not the anti-Semitism. Nothing. And if you tried, she'd simply cease listening to you until you were done.

I was a typical, apolitical New England adolescent. I didn't have much to show in the way of my personal political leanings other than a subscription to *Soldier of Fortune* magazine because I fancied the life of a mercenary. And I joined the NRA because I really liked guns, as most young men do.

Then I went to college.

It was there, with no shortage of encouragement from professors, that I developed a fairly typical worldview for an eighteen-year-old with no responsibilities other than showing up for class whenever it suited me. In short order I was to become an enlightened, overly vocal, I-have-all-the-answers kind of guy. The kind of loud, overtly political person I can't much stand now. I morphed from awkward teen to ponytailed vegan socialist animal rights activist for whom *everything* was black or white. I hated George H. W. Bush with a passion, hissing and frowning every time his mug came on TV. When I heard him complain in a debate about "card-carrying members of the ACLU" I rushed out and joined the ACLU just so I could carry one of those cards to spite him. My NRA membership lapsed and I joined People for the Ethical Treatment of Animals. I always sided with the underdog—the homeless drunk, the Palestinian militant, the murderous revolutionary. I even voted for Jesse Jackson in the 1988 primaries. Please forgive me. Please, please forgive me.

After college I entered the workforce and moved to Atlanta, a southern city that was, due to the transient nature of a lot of its population, moderately conservative in a heavily conservative region. The president was Bill Clinton and I was surrounded by people who were not at all happy about that fact. The DON'T BLAME ME, I VOTED FOR BUSH bumper stickers actually annoyed me. I loved Bill Clinton! How could you not? Whip-smart. Mischievous. Charismatic. Driven. Then came the parade of scandals: Campaign funds from China, selling the Lincoln Bedroom, the FBI files, Whitewater, his *bimbo eruptions* and the more serious allegations of rape. Then the Lewinsky scandal, the subsequent finger-in-your-face denials of it, the bombing of a Sudanese pharmaceutical factory to divert our attention from it, and the pièce de résistance, the blatantly politically motivated, incredibly shady, unpardonable pardoning of people like fugitive Marc Rich.

The love affair over, I found solace in many of the ideas held by the Libertarian Party. I developed a taste for smaller government and it took more effort to make my bleeding heart bleed. I also promised myself that from that point onward I would never again vote for the "lesser of two evils" candidate. If a party couldn't be bothered to deliver me a candidate worth voting for, they would not earn my vote. I would vote only for the candidate in whom I believed, regardless of his or her chances of winning. Despite the routine accusation that I'm "wasting" my vote I know it's the smart thing to do, like sterilizing the Kardashians is.

By the election of 2000, presented with a choice between Al Gore or George W. Bush, I lived up to that promise and found myself voting for Libertarian Party candidate Harry Browne. I knew he would not win, but Al Gore could out-wooden Pinocchio and had the stigma of the Clinton administration. Bush the Younger didn't do it for me either. Though he struck me as someone I could have a beer with, that's not necessarily the kind of guy I wanted heading the country. Plus, he didn't drink beer.

On the evening of the election I went to a Libertarian Party function. I only remember two things about that night: First, we didn't have to worry about winning, so it was a very relaxed affair. Second, some strange bearded man approached the table, placed audio cassettes on it in front of libertarian talk show host Neal Boortz and announced, "I write libertarian science fiction." That's the trouble with Libertarians. They're often just plain weird.

Hours later, having gone to bed with Al Gore the presumed winner, I awoke to "Bush Wins." I saw it as a repudiation of the Clinton years even though we now had a president who couldn't form a sentence to anyone's liking. And then, like everyone else, I watched the wrangling over the election results. As an outsider who'd voted for the obscure unknown candidate, the stakes weren't as high for me. I watched as both sides disingenuously pursued a victory. They insincerely attacked the Electoral College when it didn't work in their favor and insincerely defended it when it did. Like many of us I was disheartened at the spectacle of partisan lawyers arguing over "chads" and furious at the legal maneuvering that sought to disqualify one vote while at the same time counting another—often for the same reason. Eventually Gore was outmaneuvered and took a leave of absence from politics to go grow a beard.

It was an eye-opening experience that shook our faith in the system. Many of us Americans who had grown up believing that we had the moral authority to show other countries how democracy was done now realized we'd no longer be able to frown at the world's throne-seizing despots and tyrants and *tsk-tsk* their rigged elections and political dog-and-pony shows. The once-shining example of democracy now looked like some tin-pot banana republic, albeit one with more legal structure. Sure, we hadn't stooped to the level of stuffing ballot boxes, killing rival candidates or faking election results—but we succeeded in showing the world that underneath the surface of our successful democratic republic was an undercurrent of partisanship and cutthroat players who would do anything to win, even at the expense of democracy and the country itself. It was a pretty bad way to start the twenty-first century.

After moving to New York in September 2001 I learned that the Libertarian Party was not as well organized or serious as I had grown accustomed to it being. That became obvious during that year's mayoral election. Mike Bloomberg was the (R), Mark Green the (D). Who was the Libertarian candidate? Kenny Kramer—the inspiration for the character Kosmo Kramer on *Seinfeld*. I voted for Mike Bloomberg, who was to become a decent enough though insufferably nanny-statist mayor for whom I would not vote after he ignored the law on term limits and ran a third time in 2009.

I've since become an Independent. I have no party affiliation and I like it that way. As you'll see later on in the book, many of the Founders thought political parties were a bad idea. Give me a principled politician with views I agree with and I'll vote for him regardless of his or her party. I don't vote for the lesser of two evils, and I don't consider voting third party "wasting my vote" just because that party can't win.

To (poorly) paraphrase Martin Luther King, Jr.: Judge politicians by the content of their character, not by the capitalized letter that follows their name. In that spirit, in most cases I have refrained from slapping the party affiliation next to an individual's name in an effort to encourage you to judge them by their actions and not their political allegiance.

OK then, let's take a look at "It," shall we?

Brian Sack (Initials: B.S.)

New York City

March 2011

PART THE FIRST

These Ailing States

Wherein we take a quick look at "It"
and consider how "It" has influenced
the current condition of affairs in this country

PART THE FIRST

These Allied States

1

The Declaration of Introduction

Some self-evident truth

My fellow Americans:

Politics is like Brad Pitt. Try as you might, there's just no escaping Brad Pitt. You might not care one atom about Brad Pitt but you're exposed to Brad Pitt on a daily basis. He's on the cover of the mind-numbing glossies in the supermarket checkout line. He pops up on *Oprah* and *The View* and *Entertainment Tonight* as you scour channels in a vain search for nonreality programming. He's in the movies you watch. The conversations you overhear. He seeps into your life no matter how strongly you don't care about Brad Pitt or want to hear about Brad Pitt. You know what he looks like and when he's changed his hairstyle or shaved his goatee. You know what he sounds like. If he stood behind you and said, "Spare some change?" your immediate reaction would be, "That's not a bum's voice. That's Brad Pitt's voice."

Even though you probably do not care the slightest bit, you know Brad Pitt broke poor Jennifer Aniston's heart and fell for a woman with artificial, frightening rhinoceros lips. A scary woman who kidnaps poor black children from desolate African villages and marches around with them when cameras are pointed at her.

Brad Pitt. Brad Pitt. Brad Pitt.

Like it or not, realize it or not, Brad Pitt is omnipresent in your life.

As is politics.

You might claim to be apolitical, but technically you're not. Because you have beliefs and opinions, an idea of how you think things should be, how the world around you should function and appear. You undoubtedly have positions on a variety of issues that affect everyone on the local, national and even global level. You might choose to keep these feelings and beliefs to yourself—and thank you very much for that—but that doesn't make you apolitical. It just makes you wisely reserved and much less annoying to the six hundred complete strangers on Facebook you just added as friends.

Politics is a game that most of us do not know how to play well. And that is not a bad thing, because the game of politics is completely nonsensical to us sentient mortals. It's counterintuitive and artificial. It has bizarre rules that don't necessarily apply to the players, and rules that can be bent, broken or denied at all times. It takes insincerity to Clintonian heights and faith in humanity to Nixonian lows. Most of us are unschooled at hoarding and abusing power, stealing money, practicing hypocrisy, duplicity, lying through our teeth, manipulating fools and turning our cheeks to inexcusable malfeasance—all the while doing so under the label of *public servant*.

Calling a politician a public servant is as insulting and unsettling as Ticketmaster charging a "convenience" fee. *Bullshit.* Only in politics could you take an unconstitutional, rights-trampling, Founding Father–infuriating piece of legislative horse dung and call it the *PATRIOT* Act.

Most of us would not feel comfortable playing a game that features such constant comical absurdity delivered with straight faces. A game where oral sex isn't sex, evading military service is patriotic and saying "Read my lips . . . No new taxes!" means taxes are coming.

We'd feel bad calling the blowing up of your wedding party something as innocuous as "collateral damage." And we'd feel somewhat hypocritical about sending someone's child into harm's way while using any means available to keep our own child out of it. We don't want to kiss ugly babies, shake hands with freakish mouth-breathers or feign interest in the plight of someone facing foreclosure because they bought something they totally couldn't afford. We'd feel like hypocrites praising Jesus and marriage and family values while a hooker fellates us. By the way, that's apparently *not* sex, in case you were worried.

For most of us, politics makes very little sense because as messed up as we all are, in comparison to the people and things that live and work inside the Beltway, we are still some odd shade of normal. And that's exactly why we didn't go into politics in the first place.

Chances are we've all met a few politicians in our lives. Probably not on purpose. We know they have unnatural hair and the smiles are forced. Crocodile tears and rehearsed spontaneity. They are always weird to us, and no one is ever surprised to learn that they rank right down there with Car Dealer on lists of people you trust the least.

Most of us have a very cursory understanding of politics, of course. It's hard not to in this Information Age, where politics, like Brad Pitt, comes at us from the television, the radio, books, magazines, websites, Twitter, Facebook and overpaid actors with a tendency to opine at the Oscars.

When it comes to politics we get the gist, the same way we kind of understand algebra, or kind of understand how tornadoes form, or kind of understand the space program. It's best left to others, we'll say. And so we entrust politics to the experts, the strategists, the careerists and the political dynasties, forgetting centuries of historical precedent that suggests political genius is neither genetic nor transferable to your dependents.

But unlike algebra, tornadoes and the space program, leaving politics to the political often has a downside in that we are finding ourselves routinely, blatantly, ruthlessly and mercilessly screwed, shafted and hung out to dry by the coterie of dunderheads, ne'er-do-wells, nitwits, tyrants and filthy megalomaniacs we've entrusted to run our show.

Not understanding politics is like playing poker with people who actually know how to. Sooner or later, no matter how clever you think you may be, you're going to lose. And often. It behooves us to be a little more politically savvy, even if we're self-proclaimed nonpolitical beings. Perhaps if we knew a tad more about things—the way the system works, the people who are in the system, the damage they've done and the damage they are ultimately capable of—we'd make better moves. Maybe we wouldn't elect utter boobs, for one. Maybe we'd be able to spot terrible laws before they were rammed through both houses of Congress with a $20 billion possum ranch subsidy buried inside. Maybe we wouldn't assume that a pending bill's pleasant-sounding name had anything at all to do with the bill's terrifying content. Maybe we'd see the downside in letting the government keep sticking us with the world's biggest tab. And maybe we'd start to understand the roots of our incredible disenchantment.

So, then, let's take a look at the world of good old American politics. And let us look not through a partisan lens but through one of those fancy, higher-end objective ones. The kind that filters out as much bullshit as possible so as to give us a clear, crisp picture. Surely, that has to be a lot more interesting than Brad freaking Pitt.

Thank you, and God bless America.

2

MISERABLE AND LIED TO
Whoa, hey, why the long face?

On election night 2008, President-elect Barack Obama took to an outdoor stage in Chicago in what can only be described as an electric atmosphere. Sure, sure, there are those out there who hate the guy so much that they'd argue that the atmosphere wasn't electric, but it was. Very, very electric. Eight years of George W. Bush had taken its toll on the American psyche and a sizable chunk of the USA was well ready for Barack Obama to deliver some of that change his campaign had been advertising.

History had been made at that very moment and everyone in the country knew it and felt it and was a part of it. Even though I hadn't voted for him—or the other one, for that matter—I was excited too. Not so much at the prospect of an Obama presidency but at the realization that this country had yet again shown the world just how fantastic we were capable of being. We elected a black guy. And only four years after actor Michael Richards went on a bizarre racist rampage at the Laugh Factory comedy club. Not only that, but we elected a black guy who had a Muslim name, had practiced Islam, and whose middle name was freaking Hussein. Not too shabby only seven years after 9/11. I don't care what you think about the guy, but that's pretty damn impressive, and it says a lot about our country. Yet another bloodless transfer of power in the history of our very young country even though the stakes—heading the world's most powerful and successful nation—were so incredibly high.

We all deserve a nice pat on the back for that.

Of the people who voted that day for the first time in their lives, 71 percent voted for Obama. Energized at the prospect of kicking eight wearisome years of the Bush administration out the door, and encouraged by a get-out-the-vote campaign that seemed specifically designed to get out the Democratic vote, they'd actually registered. When November came around, they were still energized, and they headed straight to the polls. Or they were shuttled there by enthusiastic vote-getter-outers. Or they were dragged out of their homeless shelters and asylums by idealistic college kids.

Or they never existed but were registered and went to the polls anyway.

Naturally the prospect of a black president meant that record numbers of black voters had gone to the polls for the very first time as well: 95 percent of them cast their vote for Obama. So many newly registered, fresh-faced, wide-eyed voters all jumping at the chance to be part of what was shaping up to be an historical presidency, with my wife, who had just become an American citizen, among them. This kind of excitement about voting hadn't been seen since 1972, when eighteen-year-olds finally got the right to vote for or against politicians who were drafting them for Vietnam. In 2008 a whole new segment of the population was finally emancipated from decades of apathy and introduced to the fantastic world of politics.

And now they're all completely, terribly, incredibly disenchanted.

The once-enthusiastic minions we watched jumping up and down on TV that night in Chicago now mope around the water cooler, shaking their heads. They bitch communally at picnics and wedding receptions. They speak loudly of their woes at Starbucks. They sigh deeply and tell any pollster who comes calling how unsatisfied, disappointed and angry they are. As I write this particular paragraph just a few weeks before the midterm election of 2010, the atmosphere, like an Amish village, contains absolutely no electricity anymore. There's a palpable feeling of gloom.

Frankly, it's quite enjoyable for those of us who watched from the sidelines wondering why people would *ever* get so excited about a politician.

What happened between election night 2008 and now is pretty standard for those of us who have followed politics for any length of time. It's a little harder to swallow for the folks who are new to the game: the ones energized—the rest of us might say *suckered*—by the youthful exuberance, catchy campaign slogans and overall hipness of the Team Obama Campaign Machine. You couldn't help but feel sorry for the desperate and wobbling McCain, who stood in awe as Obama Twittered, Facebooked and email-blasted his way to the finish line, raking in millions like nobody's business and branding himself the bullet train to the future, as opposed to McCain's rickshaw of doom. People who had never before dabbled in politics—aside from writing "Bush Sucks" above a urinal—had been transformed into rabid evangelists, canvassers and recruiters, all emoting the kind of adoration and love for someone reminiscent of the time the Beatles played *The Ed Sullivan Show.*

Now those same people who so enthusiastically shut the door on McCain and his plucked-from-obscurity lady friend frown and shake their heads and point to the White House and ask *How come the president is not doing what he said he was going to do?*

Well, the answer is obvious to us veterans of political affairs.

We know that if presidential candidate Barack Obama had said, "I will stay in Guantánamo, Iraq and Afghanistan, I will expand upon the Constitution-shredding policies of the Bush administration, I will pay lip service to gay-marriage advocates and I will demand the unquestionable right to assassinate American citizens without due process," he would have had a much harder time getting elected. Smart politicians don't do that to themselves.

In other words, like many of us looking to get a job, he kind of lied. Does that set him apart from other candidates? *Hell, no.*

The very nature of politics lends itself to lying, since ultimately what a politician is selling is his or her very imperfect self—and you're the prospective buyer. Anyone unfortunate enough to have entered the world of online dating is well aware of the incredible amount of truth-stretching, fact-fudging and blemish-camouflaging that occurs when someone sets out to craft an appealing image of themselves for general consumption. Raging alcoholics "drink socially," the morbidly obese are "sexy," people who don't read books and who think an apostrophe is an essential part of a plural noun are "currently reading Nietzsche." The art of the self-portrait is pushed to the limits in an effort to capture the most flattering image possible by ingeniously masking height-challenged men, large-bottomed women, big noses, missing teeth and pockmarked skin. Whatever it takes to make a sale and land an evening out.

So, yes, a politician is of the same mind-set and practicing the same techniques as someone looking to get lucky on Match.com. The only difference is that the politician isn't just looking for a one-night stand: They're hoping you'll stick around so they can keep screwing you for as long as possible. I take that back. It's a one-vote stand. And if they score, you might not hear from them for four years.

Lying is simply par for the course in politics. The excited new voters of 2008 might not have known this, but now they do. If we've lived through even one political campaign we've come to expect it of our candidates. When Hillary Clinton dons a Yankees cap and tells us she's always been a big fan, there's not a single sensible one among us who nods our head in agreement, because we know she's completely and utterly full of shit. Likewise, when Sarah Palin stares off into the horizon after being asked what newspapers she reads, and twenty to thirty minutes later replies "all of 'em"—we don't waste a fraction of a second contemplating her answer because we simply know it's not true. Even someone with a vested interest in Clinton or Palin being elected to office, for whatever reasons they might have, knows these people are simply not being truthful. The politician's sole goal is to earn our vote by telling us what we want to hear. Anyone who's ever lured someone to bed with the false promise of a long-term relationship should totally understand.

While we admonish our own children and spouses for lying, we're remarkably forgiving of our politicians—especially if the lie is of any potential benefit to our own political leanings. That naked hypocrisy is all too common in politics today and we'll address that later in the book.

That our politicians are compulsive, unapologetic, blatant liars is so commonly understood and expected that when a politician who *doesn't* lie rears his head, it's remarkably noticeable. It's also usually disastrous. When New York gubernatorial candidate Carl Paladino told us that he had a bastard child with a mistress and that gays are dysfunctional, we were momentarily refreshed and even entertained by his unexpected honesty.

But with his campaign in free fall it was clear that he probably should have lied, just like every other politician does.

SPARE SOME CHANGE

So now we have a steady stream of voters new to politics who have been baptized by ire. They've climbed down the ladder from their postelection cloud nine to voice their frustrations and complaints about the way things are going. They do it on message boards and via Twitter and through Facebook and all the other work-avoidance media of the day. *This is not what I signed up for,* they groan. *Things were supposed to be different by now.*

They are different, in the sense that we have a president who's intellectual and can form a complete sentence. But things are not different, in the sense that the issues that people were protesting about in 2008 are still issues. But those people who were protesting then have their guy in the Oval Office now. So now they're annoyed. And they're really disenchanted. There are new people protesting now, and they seem to be annoyed and disenchanted too, but the people who put their guy in the Oval Office can't seem to pinpoint exactly what the new protesters are annoyed and disenchanted about.

The downside of a slick and well-run political campaign is that when you offer a smorgasbord of promises and don't deliver abundantly or quickly, reality sinks in. A lot of those people who responded to your call to arms get understandably upset. If you tell a young man he gets seventy-two hotties in paradise for blowing himself up in a café—there's no repercussion when you don't deliver. You can continue to snicker and recruit horny zealots as it suits you.

But politics deals with the here and now, and the repercussions are felt in the here and now as well.

The disenchantment prompts people to introspection and a review of the reasons they were so energized to vote in the first place. They start to calculate the promises made versus those delivered upon. And then in the most telling sign, the media that had once acted as uncritical cheerleader begins to instead critique and reevaluate. And thus, resentment grows, so that when you come around the next time asking constituents to go to the polls on your behalf, they tell you to go take a hike. In fact, in the run-up to the midterm 2010 election, the sense of desperation on the part of the Democrats was clear, with everyone from the president on down begging their angry party members to go to the polls and keep the dream alive—all but offering them a ride on Air Force One if that's what it would take. They gave it their best, but 29 million of the voters who showed up on Election Day 2008 apparently had better things to do on Election Day 2010.

Perhaps, in between elections, those voters had learned that politicians are like frozen pizza: The picture on the box always looks better than what comes out of the oven. And sometimes, when you go for another brand, you get the same lousy pizza in a different box.

WELCOME TO THE MALAISE

For the newly despondent, the recently disenchanted, we can put our arms around them, pull them close and offer some consolation: We've all been there. We all know what they're going through. We can let them know they're not alone. Every one of us at one time or another was wide-eyed and trusting of the people for whom we voted, only to have our heart tossed off a cliff to the rocks below.

Do you remember where you were the day you realized Mel Gibson was an asshole? I don't either. But I remember the terrible feeling of betrayal. I remember the realization that someone I'd invested a lot of time in admiring and liking didn't deserve it—at all. You encounter that feeling a lot in politics.

With politicians, eventually some series of events—or sometimes just one really big one—shakes us from our obliviousness and self-imposed denial and forces us to confront the truth: that all politicians are simply prone to disappoint us, good ones and bad ones alike. It took some time for folks to come to realize that Bill Clinton was a shady, opportunistic sociopath with a penchant for sexual assault or that George W. Bush was as fiscally conservative as Paris Hilton on a coke bender.

But we got there—with both of them.

So let's admit that when it comes to politics, those of us who have partaken are all varying stages of miserable. Our misery level waxes and wanes depending on numerous factors, such as the outcome of the most recent election and which way our favorite legislation seems to be headed, but the more involved in politics we are, the less likely we are to be happy about it. After all, politics is ultimately the art of telling people what they can and must and cannot and won't do. For that reason alone, very little good can come of it.

People really hate being told things like that.

TREATING DEPRESSION

So what can we do to make ourselves feel better? What's the best way to go about addressing this malaise that's set in? Acknowledging the problem is a great start, and it seems like we might be doing just that: finally breaking away from the partisan in us and realizing that there's no shortage of awful in politics across the spectrum. Realizing that different parties bring different bullshit to the table whether they're Democrats, Republicans, Independents, Libertarians, Greens or Luddite Vegan Anarchists. It's all bad.

Demanding more from our politicians and their masters would certainly be a good start. Imagine if our esteemed political strategists and campaign managers could no longer rely on their base to impulsively support whatever crap sandwich of a candidate they presented to us. Imagine if we refused to simply cast a vote out of some nonsensical, thoughtless allegiance to a party and instead demanded our DNCs, RNCs, Roves, Penns and Carvilles stop insulting us with their constant lesser-of-two-evils options and strategic-but-unqualified candidates.

What if we were *all* swing voters? What if you weren't praised for announcing that you've only ever voted the Republican or Democratic ticket your whole life, but rather you were derided for taking a lame cop-out.

What does party loyalty get you anyway? It gets you the right to stand in front of the Kerry/Edwards or Bush/Cheney levers and realize "This kind of sucks."

We *know* there's a problem. We *know* we're miserable. We're tired of the lies. We want to feel better. Acknowledging all that is a fantastic step in the right direction. But we also have to understand something else:

We're all full of crap too.

3

PARTISAN AND MISINFORMED
Loudest one wins, right?

The rise of partisanship in this country could probably best be explained with the use of Al Gore's famous hockey stick graph. It's no secret that throughout history politics has always managed to send one group or another stomping off in a huff, but it would seem we're currently experiencing peak levels of rabid, screamy-yelly, I-hate-your-opinion partisanship. Hordes of highly energized *politizoids* patrolling the streets, airwaves and cybertubes, on a perpetual war footing, eager to unleash salvo upon salvo of bitter Hate-orade upon any poor soul unfortunate enough to have a differing opinion and to commit the terrible crime of offering it up . . . something our Founding Fathers actually thought would be a good idea.

When Dixie Chicks front woman Natalie Maines voiced her opinion of George W. Bush and the pending Iraq War to a London audience in 2003, she quickly came to understand that freedom of speech came with a downside. With the kind of ferocity usually reserved for Islamic mobs protesting cartoons, red-state America went absolutely apeshit. Maines could only watch helplessly as, in a no-holds-barred frenzy, half her audience took a hike, the phone rang with death threats and piles of Dixie Chicks CDs were bulldozed at rallies. She and her band were called every conceivable name in the book, from the brainless vulgar ones to the eerie political ones that suggest one should be exiled, or shot: words like *traitor* and *un-American*. Really? Because she didn't think we should go to war? Yes, apparently. Mind you, it wasn't like she was sharing an unpopular opinion: At least half of her country agreed with her, as did most of the countries we'd consider allies. And most of the countries we *don't* consider allies too.

I'm no expert in country music by any means but I know there are several artists of that genre who sing songs about America being totally awesome. If one were to choose to punish Ms. Maines for her opinion, would it not be a sufficient punishment to divert the funds for one's next CD purchase toward one of countrydom's rah-rah-the-U.S.A.-is-great performers instead? No, in these partisan times she needed to be absolutely torn to shreds for her audacious and unacceptable display of opinion-having.

Her real crime was in not understanding the partisan political leanings of her audience and not pandering to them, even though she was an addressing an audience in London that wholeheartedly agreed with her. She'd be advised to learn from masters like the insufferable Kanye West, who prompted cheers by telling his audience that George Bush hated black people (despite Bush, at the time, having the most diverse cabinet in American history). The two have since reconciled, with Bush 43 describing that moment as an "all time low" in his presidency. If absolutely nothing worse happened for George between 2000–2008, then not bothering to read *Decision Points* was definitely a good decision point on my behalf.

With so many folks primed to attack, you need to be careful what you say. You also need to be careful of what you *don't* say.

Lawrence Summers attended MIT at sixteen years old and followed up that impressive credit with a doctorate from Harvard University—an educational background that should make any aspiring intellectual terribly jealous. Certainly someone who accomplished that and then went on to become one of the youngest tenured professors in Harvard's history is smart, right? Did I mention he then became Harvard's twenty-seventh president? Very, very smart guy, right? No! He is a stupid, stupid, ignorant, dum-dum-pants! At least, that was the verdict of everyone who took offense to a few out-of-context lines in a speech he made. What did this incredibly educated but apparently unforgivably stupid person do? In observation of the fact that women were not very well represented in the highest levels of science and engineering, he offered up three hypotheses to explain that fact. One hypothesis, unfortunately for him, was that it's possible that women don't have the same aptitude as men on that end of the science and engineering spectrum. Does this mean that he was actually hoping that this explained the state of things—that he was rooting for women's being underrepresented in science and engineering because they weren't as good at it? Did he say women were dumb? Should stay in the kitchen? No, it was merely a hypothesis, one of three he offered. Simply a proposition to explain something worthy of being investigated further. Did that matter to the now-mobilized and totally outraged hordes of predominantly left-leaning, Lawrence Summers–hating crusaders? Nope, not a bit.

The narrative of choice was that Dr. Larry had said women were too dumb for science, and therefore he was a sexist, misogynist white guy. Attempts to apologize for the misunderstanding and explain came to naught. The Harvard faculty voted "no confidence" just to make sure he understood that he was all alone, and he resigned the following year.

So what has this mindless, knee-jerk partisanship taught us? Well, for starters: *Shut your mouth if it's not what I want to hear.* Suddenly everyone's tripping over themselves to avoid saying the "wrong" thing, doing whatever it takes to prevent themselves from getting labeled, burned in effigy or fired. But if public debate serves the public interest and is absolutely essential for successfully addressing all the complex issues we face in a democracy, are we not setting ourselves up for a wee bit of trouble?

Dissent or critical thinking shouldn't be chased off a cliff by a pitchfork-and-torch-wielding mob. But it is, and all too often. What's worse is understanding that if Ms. Maines were to tell an audience anywhere in the world that she was ashamed of President Obama and his foreign policy, the very same people calling for her head in 2003 would be scooping up her CDs and praising her for being an outspoken American. Had Lawrence Summers instead hypothesized that white males were less scientifically apt, the very same people who called for his head would have cheered him for his intellectual brilliance.

In other words: There's way too much bullshit right about now.

Which begs the question: *Why?*

What fuels the partisan mob and helps them light their torches?

THE MISINFORMATION SUPERHIGHWAY

Never before have we been so connected to the world's marketplace of ideas. And this massive marketplace of ideas doesn't have any quality control, like Williams-Sonoma or L.L. Bean does. It's more like an unregulated Moroccan bazaar—people with wares to sell, and people looking for something to buy. With two billion people on the Internet, there are a lot of thoughts, opinions and ideas for sale. And just like any yard sale, there are the occasional gems surrounded by incredible amounts of crap.

The amazing technology of the Internet puts us only a mouse click away from copious amounts of information. Information that's good, bad, unsourced, hearsay, mean-spirited, well intentioned, misleading, slightly wrong, correct, deplorable, out of context, brilliant, frightening, nonsensical, thought-provoking and pointless. Anyone with an inbox has likely received a slew of forwarded emails, many of which have a political bent and subject titles like "Our Commander-in-Chief can't even do the pledge of allegiance!" (In that particular instance, it's a photo that was flipped around so as to show the president holding the wrong hand over his heart.) We believe the ones we want to believe—the ones that suit our political frame of mind and instinctively forward them unvetted to friends and relatives, business associates and even strangers, adding our own little comments like "Can you believe this guy? Outrageous!"

Websites such as Snopes.com, FactCheck.org, PolitiFact.com and others exist solely to debunk the gigabytes of nonsense flying around cyberspace. But it's a Sisyphean task because in the time it takes people to actually fact-check an email they've received—in order to discover it's not even slightly grounded in the truth—the same email has already been forwarded to three hundred more people. And so the cycle continues, with nonsense spreading like an oil slick across the globe, coating and suffocating everything in its way until no one knows up from down.

BARACKMUSLIMOBAMAISCONTROLLEDBYGAYALIENS.COM

If you believe anything, there's a website to cater to it. And if there isn't you can start one for a pittance. With the free templates and do-it-yourself websites you can be up and running in ten minutes with a potential audience of millions. You needn't have a clue what you're talking about; there's no barrier to entry. Whether you believe that we never landed on the moon, that the president is from Kenya, that Democrats are a fifth column of Soviets, that Jesus walked with the dinosaurs or that Bobby Kennedy killed Marilyn—well, you're free to get out there and make it available to the masses. And I guarantee you, as long as it's not too outlandish—and that takes a lot these days—there's someone who'll take you up on it, believe it and without hesitation gladly repost it as fact somewhere else to help spread the good word.

Anyone with a journalistic bent can disseminate news on a wide scale, regardless of their credentials or academic background. Self-appointed media watchdogs like the left-leaning Media Matters or the right-leaning Andrew Breitbart spend their days rummaging through the hampers of their ideological enemies, eager to find a piece of dirty laundry that they can then wave around as they scream "Gotcha!" And if they can't find it, they're not beyond taking some clean laundry and describing it in the vilest way possible and hoping you'll take it as dirty. If it works, it works, and if it falls flat, well, there's always tomorrow.

These organizations and websites often have a clearly stated agenda that one might presume would affect their reportage, but that never seems to be a concern—provided the information they offer suits the reader's palate. The comments sections of these websites ultimately become insular communities of like-minded individuals where anyone audacious enough to offer up a contrary view quickly finds themselves in the same predicament as a germ surrounded by white blood cells. Having been thusly savaged, the intruder moves on and finds a website more to his liking.

Anyone of a moderate political disposition quickly learns to keeps his opinions to himself, unless he derives some kind of pleasure from being savaged by the commentariat.

It comes as no surprise, then, that in an atmosphere of uncritical thinking, within these petri dishes of polarized thought, even the most outlandish ideas and beliefs can be synthesized and flourish until they break loose and find themselves borne into the mainstream. And then, *voilà,* one more item gets added to the litany of ingrained untruths that everyone else must then devote time to rebutting, denying and responding to—with the usual ugly consequences.

DISLIKE

Social networks like Facebook introduce us to a universe of people with a world of opinions on anything and everything under the sun. Emboldened by the anonymity and buffer zone that the Internet provides, we feel free to leap into discussions on all matters political, offering our own opinions on subjects we often know little to nothing about, backing them up not with facts but with *passion.* Insults fly freely—because you can't get punched through your laptop—and sides are taken. Others leap in to the fracas, hear-hearing, digitally high-fiving, adding their own lack of understanding to the commentary, or cutting and pasting talking points from their favorite pundits. Nothing is actually learned or resolved, there's never an "Oh, I see your point" moment. Best-case scenario, everyone agrees to disagree. But the usual outcome is a flurry of indignation, insult and eye-rolling before everyone moves on to the next battle, even more partisan than they were before and thoroughly convinced that liberals are arrogant, pompous asses and conservatives are mouth-breathing idiots.

Less confrontational types needn't be kept out of the loop either. They can passive-aggressively link to items or "like" them on Facebook subtly letting folks know where they stand without actually having to come out and say it.

THE TERROR OF THE COMMENTARIAT

Someday in the future a clever scientist will calculate exactly how much time and energy has been wasted in the comment sections on the Internet, where individuals with nothing to gain from actually doing so engage in open warfare that leaves the outside observer despondent over the deplorable state of the country. The scientist will publish his findings and we will all weep and weep and weep at what could have been accomplished had all that time and energy been directed toward something more useful; a mission to Mars perhaps.

Comment sections are like the Wild West. But instead of guns people carry half-assed knowledge of history and callous disregard for the rules of grammar. It's a very scary place, and if you spend too long there, you're tainted. So in that sense it's a lot like Washington, D.C. Just like D.C., it's mostly politics. And if you spend any time there at all you know it can get ugly fast.

Name-calling is par for the course. If one's argument lacks substance they merely toss in vulgarities like *libtard* or *teabagger* to drive the point home—the point being they don't like your opinion. No provocation is necessary, because even politely disagreeing with someone is an invitation to an ad hominem attack: the declaration that you're an idiot, a pawn, a nutjob, a commie, a sheep, a Nazi and then some. Did you have the audacity to suggest ObamaCare seemed like a bad idea? Then you're a "typical wingnut douchebag." Were you foolish enough to point out something the Obama administration did right? "Keep drinking that Obamunist Kool-Aid, dipshit."

Unlike the academic debates you may have experienced in high school or college, Internet debates aren't too big on preparation. There's no stack of note cards. No one has actually practiced. And there's certainly no one moderating. Did you expect someone to actually read an article before commenting on it? They didn't. The mere assumption of what an article is about and what biases it must have is reason enough for the partisan sort to remove the safety and start firing off a missive that has absolutely nothing to do with the matter at hand. Reading takes time but opining is easy.

The Internet turns us all into New York City cabdrivers, free to roughly paraphrase what we believe we heard on a favorite talk show or think we read in an article. Not knowing what they are talking about has never, in the history of the Internet, prevented someone from offering their take on the matter. That's how we wind up with commentariat gems like "Hitler, Mussilini [*sic*] and Stalin were trying to create a pure race of Aryan people."

The commenter can't spell Mussolini and thinks the Axis powers were all part of the Aryan race, but offered her opinion up for the masses anyway. Even better, this masterpiece was evacuated from the bowels of the writer's keyboard into the comment section of an article about the 1944 Warsaw Uprising of Poland's Home Army against the Germans—where it didn't really belong. The commentariat, either unwilling to read the article or incapable of understanding it, had decided that the article was instead about the Holocaust and the completely unrelated Warsaw Ghetto Uprising by Jews in 1943. Some poor bastard who tried to point that important fact out and redirect the conversation was quickly labeled an anti-Semite and torn to shreds by the mob. And so it goes.

Really, unless you're a masochist who enjoys devoting valuable time to a worthless endeavor you'd be much better off forgoing any and all comment sections in favor of a long shower or repainting the kitchen.

A LITTLE BIRDIE TOLD ME YOU SUCK

As if the curse of bulk email forwarding, Facebook, hundreds of thousands of websites and the wretched cacophony of the commentariat weren't enough—along comes Twitter. A brilliant if not unprofitable innovation that was quickly seized upon to make us even more bitter, uninformed and partisan than we already were. Through the magic of this medium one can easily broadcast—sorry, tweet—any rumination one has to an audience of anywhere from zero to millions. As long as it's under 140 characters, of course. Fortunately, when you don't know what you're talking about, their brevity mandate comes in handy.

Twitter allows us to follow our heroes' thoughts and feelings, lets them direct us to their favorite articles and YouTube videos and even contact them directly in the hopes they might acknowledge us and respond back. More often than not, when we try to contact celebrities through Twitter we get the same result as if we'd just shouted 140 characters at our TV set.

By virtue of Twitter's ease of use and its direct connection to followers, there's no publicist to filter what the celebrity thinks before he or she hits a button and the celebrity's thoughts (or, often, lack thereof) reaches his or her adoring fans. That allows the more outspoken Twitterati to swiftly and thoughtlessly share their political opinions with people who then agree—or hate them. Through this medium I've learned that film critic Roger Ebert is tremendously partisan (though to his credit he refrains from the vulgarity *teabagger* and uses *teepee* instead). I also know that Scott Baio hates the Obama administration, and actor John Cusack is more left-wing and less literate than I'd hoped.

This does great things for partisanship.

But Twitter isn't limited to movers and shakers or celebrities—it's the great egalitarian sentiment-sharing machine. We too can play, and should a random thought occur to us, an article pique our interest, or someone offend us with his or her views, we can jump into this community—firing off links and opinions and insults just like the rest of them. Behold these real tweets:

- Bill O'Reilly makes me sick.
- Keith Olbermann is a moronic, anti-Christian bigot, seditious, inbred ingrate, cynical, sarcastic, pompous ass.
- Is it bad that I am disappointed that Glenn Beck doesn't have cancer?

In effect, Twitter turns us all into mean-spirited comedians and political pundits. As if we didn't have enough already.

ENOUGH?

Fed as we are on a daily diet of this stuff, we've lost the capacity to reason, to critically assess, to separate the wheat from the chaff. It's our way or the highway, and if someone's message doesn't gel with our worldview, we're primed to accuse the messenger not the message. They're biased, dishonest, an idiot, a fool. It doesn't matter what degrees they may have from whatever prestigious universities; it doesn't matter if they've got a storied background in whatever they're talking about: *they know nothing*. Fingers in ears, nyahnyah-nyah.

How refreshing it would be to engage in a discussion wherein intelligent points are made, real facts are presented and the discourse remains civil, friendly and conducted using the indoor voice. Perhaps these discussions could contain an occasional concession here or there as in "I see what you're saying" or "You have a very good point." Perhaps, even when both sides vehemently disagree, it could end with "Well, I beg to differ" or even "Let's agree to disagree" rather than "You teabagging moron" or "You gay libtard." I'm not asking that we return to the Victorian days of absurdly proper behavior, starched collars and calling cards—but Jiminy Christmas, these screaming matches and cyberscuffles are making us all miserable.

The Internet is an amazing creation in many ways, but as is the human tendency, we've taken this extraordinary technology and made its primary function the dissemination of pornography followed closely with the complete dumbing down of the agitated masses.

Part the Second

Background Check

Wherein we take a look at the history of this country
so as to better understand "It"

4

THE U.S. CONSTITUTION

Short, intelligent and often misunderstood—
like Prince

WE THE PEOPLE

The Constitution, like Michael Jackson, has an older and less successful brother: the Articles of Confederation. The Articles established a new American government and how it would be run, but not long after doing so, the Founders and their cohorts started having regrets about some of the decisions they'd made in putting that document together. In the same way we can imagine George Lucas saying, "Jar Jar Binks was probably a bad idea," we can imagine Sam Adams or Patrick Henry lamenting how the Articles gave every state one vote in a Congress that required unanimous votes to do anything. In effect, with the Articles as they were, every state had veto power over the national government and could conceivably hold legislation hostage for whatever reasons might arise. Not exactly a

31

recipe for getting much done. That oversight plus several other flaws made the Articles less than ideal for a fledgling republic. It wasn't long before the Founders started to nitpick the thing, much like you do when trying to wean yourself off a significant other whom you've lost interest in: "She has cankles. She clicks when she chews. She doesn't have a bicameral legislature."

To be fair, it's not the Articles of Confederation's fault. It's us. She was put together hastily, while the Revolution was still going on and British people were shooting at us.

George Lucas, on the other hand, has absolutely no excuse for Jar Jar Binks.

So the Founders, having learned a few lessons from their first stab at the government-establishing game, set about discussing and drafting the Constitution of the United States of America. In a room. In the middle of summer. With the windows shut to ensure privacy. It's a wonder that our founding document isn't just a string of heat-related expletives with a declaration that we have an inalienable right to air-conditioning.

It would be hard to re-create that endeavor today and not just because we don't seem as smart as those guys anymore. Imagine the shitstorm of protest that would ensue if a group of white males were to announce that they were going to lock themselves in a room and come up with a blueprint for the country. For starters, they'd be pilloried for their lack of religious and ethnic diversity. Not to mention the fact that in this day and age everyone considers themselves an expert in everything and would be eager to offer their input and expect it be taken into serious consideration. Can you imagine how long that would take? Nearly an entire decade passed after 9/11 before we finally, kind of, agreed on a plan for rebuilding the World

Trade Center site, so just try to envision how long it would take us to put together a Constitution: one written by the same people who fill Internet comment threads with their half-assed opinions, ignorance of history, mindless drivel and absolutely stunning grammatical shortcomings.

But 230 years ago there was not much diversity. Certainly not enough worth celebrating. A bunch of straight white Euro guys in a room was pretty much the norm. Political Correctness had yet to be invented. Really, they had to appease just themselves. That freed them to develop a brilliant document that has stood the test of time. And we love it. Boy, do we love it.

We love the Constitution so much that we want everyone else in the whole wide world to love it just as much as we do. In fact, I believe most Americans are under the impression that this is the only country with a constitution. For that reason we often find ourselves entering other countries, propping up their insane, dysfunctional governments and coaching them to write a slightly customized version of our Constitution. "Try this," we tell them as if it were a cool mixtape. "It's awesome."

Inevitably we find ourselves profoundly disappointed that their insane, dysfunctional, medieval kleptocracy was unable to transition smoothly from government-by-warlord to one that embraced our noble democratic principles. We shrug our shoulders, hop in our tanks and rumble off to proselytize elsewhere. Then the warlords go back to government-by-warlord and promptly set about killing everyone who listened to our mixtape.

The Constitution created the federal government of the United States of America—and did so with remarkably few words. In fact, at four pages it's shorter than the assembly instructions for an Ikea night table. Better yet, despite its brevity it managed to create the world's longest-enduring constitutional republic, one that has lasted hundreds of years longer than an Ikea night table ever will.

Little did they know that this brief document they were signing would birth a government that would eventually create an incomprehensible tax code that numbers around eighty thousand pages on a good day. If only tax laws were written by the Founding Fathers. Can you imagine what the Constitution would look like if it were written by today's crop of babbling, verbose, ineloquent "let's just ratify this sucker and find out what it says later" legislators?

Although we have a tendency to lionize the men who created the Constitution, they certainly were extremely clever. Many people see them as being ahead of their time in creating a document that was so simple yet so solid, uncanny in its ability to thwart the human tendency to accidentally ruin a good thing and prescient in its ability to adapt to what Donald Rumsfeld might have called the *known unknowns* of the future. They seem one step ahead of us, prepared for the many eventualities that could and would arise. Their descendants are probably the kind of folks who always have an umbrella somewhere on hand and who plot their vacation itineraries down to the minute rather than grabbing an outdated guidebook and winging it like the rest of us.

The men who created the Constitution were very wary of the consolidation of power. They didn't trust people with it. The English monarchy they broke from had left them with political posttraumatic stress disorder. They deliberately installed safeguards that effectively made acquiring too much power as difficult as firing a semiliterate, unionized teacher. These checks and balances helped to distribute power and ensure the viability of the document and the longevity of the government it created. In other words—without the distractions of the Internet, Netflix, TiVo and Xbox Live, these men were able to craft something that was farsighted and extraordinarily brilliant.

SHORT AND SWEET

The Constitution is only four pages long, serving as testament to the brains, clarity and talent for succinctness that the Founding Fathers possessed. An entire government, one that would eventually become a superpower no less, was created with a document shorter than a prenuptial agreement between Mark Sanford and some unfortunate Argentinean tart.

It created the House of Representatives and the Senate, the Supreme Court and the office of the president. It provides for the defense of the member states and in general lives up to what it set out to do in the preamble:

We the People of the United States, in Order to form a more perfect Union, establish Justice, insure domestic Tranquility, provide for the common defence, promote the general Welfare, and secure the Blessings of Liberty to ourselves and our Posterity, do ordain and establish this Constitution for the United States of America . . . Yadda, yadda, yadda and they're done. No pandering to lobbyists or special interest groups, no baffling legalese, no pseudo-intellectual jargon, no asterisks directing you to enormous blocks of legally required disclaimers. Four pages and done. And even better—in case they missed something—they detailed the process for amending the document later. A process that's no walk in the park, for certain, yet still seems easier than amending a document in Microsoft Word.

The Constitution can be amended but doing so takes two-thirds of each house of Congress. Getting that kind of cooperation in such a nasty, partisan atmosphere is as difficult as coaxing a sincere smile out of Senator John Kerry. That kind of difficulty is completely, utterly, totally on purpose because the Founding Fathers in all their eighteenth-century wisdom knew that left to their own devices, someone in the future would come along and likely fuck it all up.

OH, PROBABLY WORTH MENTIONING

There was some concern that the Constitution wasn't clear enough on how it empowered the people. Three years after the Constitution was ratified came the first ten amendments. The intention was to clarify what powers the government *did not* have. These amendments were gathered into what is called the Bill of Rights and they are the most cited, misunderstood and sometimes confusing amendments of the lot. They are the following:

THE FIRST AMENDMENT

I Love You, You're Perfect, Now Change

> Congress shall make no law respecting an establishment of religion, or prohibiting the free exercise thereof; or abridging the freedom of speech, or of the press; or the right of the people peaceably to assemble, and to petition the Government for a redress of grievances.

For all the talk of their complete and undying love for the Constitution many Americans seem to have a hard time totally committing to it. *You're the one for me . . . but we should see other people on occasion.* Even our elected officials who take the fairly straightforward oath to "uphold and defend the Constitution" seem to develop issues when it comes to actually upholding and defending the Constitution. This imperfect relationship is due in part to people not completely understanding the document that they love so very much, and also misunderstanding it. It is very apparent that some people either do not realize or do not like that the First Amendment also protects lots of *things you may not like.*

Freedom of speech, which the First Amendment was so nice to provide us, is often misunderstood by people as the freedom to say and do things *as long as they don't hurt my feelings.* Unfortunately for those of this mind-set, and fortunately for liberty as a whole, there's nothing that protects you from free speech that you find offensive. People cannot pick and choose the opinions and ideas they're willing to tolerate and the ones they want shushed. In a culture used to getting its way all the time, that can be a hard pill to swallow. Stories of this tug-of-war between people speaking freely and people who mistakenly believe they have the freedom to not be offended can be found all too often in the news. Usually they're small battles—in the form of a student not allowed to wear a particular T-shirt to school, or a debate being shouted down or canceled altogether because of unruly protesters. But every so often the issue gets really, really huge. And oddly enough fire seems to be involved. *Examples?* Sure!

TRAMPLING OLD GLORY TO SAVE IT

Republicans love America and the Constitution and they want you to know that they love America and the Constitution much, much, ever so much more than those lousy Democrats. In fact, they'll have you know they love America so much that they'd rather rip their beloved Constitution to shreds than let you express yourself by burning the country's flag. Sure, they totally understand that the Constitution grants you freedom of speech and expression but when it comes to flags? *Flags don't count.* Flags are off limits because the flag represents the great country that grants you the freedom of speech and expression you're . . . trying to utilize.

Now, you don't have to be a constitutional scholar to understand that the Constitution allows you to burn a flag—because that fact was pointed out for you by the Supreme Court in 1989 and 1990. But it still doesn't stop the I-love-America-so-much brigade from trying again and again to prove that they love the Constitution's freedoms so much that they're going to change the Constitution to limit them.

The Republican leadership seems to get especially worked up about this when a good hot-button issue is needed to rally the electorate. In 2000 a constitutional flag-burning amendment failed. In 2006, Senator Orrin Hatch tried once again. Senator Mel Martinez gave a thumbs-up to Hatch's amendment proposal, declaring, "All rights enshrined in the Constitution have certain limits." Uh huh. Well, let's all gather round the campfire and be totally honest with one another: Just how fast and far do you think Senator Martinez ("A" rated by the NRA) would flee from "All rights enshrined in the Constitution have certain limits" if instead of Freedom of Speech you went and tried to apply his theory to the Second Amendment?

Guess it depends on what your definition of *certain limits* is.

The 2006 amendment proposal came up for a vote just prior to the midterm elections. That'd be midterm elections where people were upset about George W. Bush, wars in Iraq and Afghanistan, rising gas prices and a growing deficit. The cynical among us might be inclined to believe that the Republicans used flag burning as a distraction that summer in an effort to rally their base to show up to the polls. Or perhaps that had nothing to do with it and Orrin Hatch is such a patriot that he simply wanted to forbid something the Founding Fathers allowed.

Regardless of the motivations, the idea that you would amend the Constitution to forbid something you don't like sucks. It also shows profound ignorance of the Constitution's original purpose of granting and protecting your freedoms—not taking them away.

Fortunately, the 2006 amendment failed—but not by a lot. You can be certain some politician somewhere will try again—and that he will be a Republican who loves his country *so much*. It will most likely happen in a year when the Republicans are getting hammered in the polls and need to get folks riled up.

Assuming you're a rational person and can entertain this topic without changes in skin tone, spittle and teeth-gritting, here's where being able to balance your emotion and your logic comes in: If you're like many Americans, the idea of someone burning the flag elicits an emotional response. It quite possibly pisses you off, and frankly it should. It's a very unpleasant symbolic gesture because you love what the flag represents, even if the flag itself was made in China. Pissing you off is *exactly* why some jackass would set fire to the flag in the first place—whether they're in Gaza, Islamabad or Berkeley.

Now, setting the emotional response aside, you need to now consider the logical aspect of this: Acknowledging that people in this country have the right to do something is *not the same* as endorsing what they're doing. Most people would agree that burning the flag is pretty reprehensible. Not to mention it contributes to greenhouse gases, which makes Al Gore cry.

One is reminded of the quote: "I disagree with what you're

saying, but I'll defend to the death your right to say it." That's the attitude that makes this country, for all its faults, a great one.

Hawaiian senator and one-armed veteran Daniel Inouye summed it up quite nicely during the most recent attempt to ban flag burning: "I believe Americans gave their lives in the many wars to make certain that all Americans have a right to express themselves, even those who harbor hateful thoughts."

Most of us have seen the "Freedom Isn't Free" bumper stickers. We all understand that it refers to the cost in blood that's been spilled in the defense and protection of our democracy. But it also applies to the horrible, horrible "God Hates Fags" people as well as some eighteen-year-old halfwit torching Old Glory: Sometimes freedom costs us in the form of suffering unpleasant things when we'd rather not.

ANGRY, ANGRY HYPOCRITES

Now, we've picked on the right a bit because they've spearheaded some of the most aggressive attempts to prohibit freedom of speech in the name of defending the Constitution. But the left has done more than its fair share of First Amendment–forgetting. Most recently, in fall 2010, shortly ahead of the ninth anniversary of 9/11. Florida pastor Terry Jones—a nobody with a large mustache, weird church and a flock of only thirty or so—decided he needed some publicity. So he passed around a press release announcing his intention to burn Islam's holy book, the Koran. Normally a stupid stunt like this would have been ignored, his fax tossed into the trash at various news bureaus and Jones would have had to think of something more clever than that. Alas, Pastor Jones had two things going in his favor:

1. It was a slow news week.
2. Everyone is terribly, terribly afraid of Islam.

Again, yet another situation that begs you to evaluate it logically—with the clarity of thought you can have when you're able to shelve your emotions for a moment. Unfortunately, fear clouded everyone's judgment—and then some—and many people came to the conclusion: *No! He can't do that!*

Of course, they were wrong. He *can* (and eventually did) do that, no matter how angry or scared it makes you feel. It's protected by the Constitution that Americans of all stripes claim to love. That didn't stop President Obama from weighing in and advising against it, or a U.S. general in Afghanistan from openly worrying that it would only place our troops in danger.

It's worth noting that our troops are already in danger by virtue of being in *Afghanistan,* where they have been since 2001.

When the president steps in to tell you not to exercise your First Amendment right—well, that's weird. Not to say that burning the Koran wasn't a silly provocation, and it's certainly offensive to the followers of Islam who aren't terrorists (there are plenty, really). But it's protected speech whether you like it or not. And just because you know that lots of bored Muslims in foreign lands will take umbrage and go ballistic and set fire to embassies and possibly each other, it is no reason to forsake our Constitution. But that's exactly what happened, and shame on everyone who meddled.

Presumably you remember the Muhammad cartoon controversy—the Danish one, not the *South Park* one. Outraged at the cartoon depiction in 2005 of their Prophet, numerous ambassadors and representatives from Islamic countries angrily demanded that Danish prime minister Anders Fogh Rasmussen apologize on behalf of Denmark and *Jyllands-Posten,* the newspaper that published the cartoons. His response was something a Founding Father might have said—except the guy is Danish and his middle name is Fogh. He said: "In Denmark, we do not apologize for having freedom of speech."

Whoa, hey! Instant citizenship for that guy. Anyone who appreciated Freedom of Speech trumping indignation and self-censorship cheered at that moment. After years of watching our politicians hem and haw when it came to sticking up for the Constitution, here was one who actually got it. So what if he was Danish.

It's worth noting that no paper in the United States, United Kingdom or Canada had the intestinal fortitude to reprint the cartoons in question. So, the Constitution can give you the rights to freedom of speech and expression but it clearly can't give you the *cojones* to actually exercise them.

THE REST OF THE FIRST

You wouldn't know it from all the invokers of the First Amendment who seem to believe that it's solely about free speech, but the amendment also guarantees the right of freedom of press, religion and assembly. And the right to complain to government to get its act together. This one amendment ensures that magazines like *Mother Jones* or *National Review* can write scathing articles about the president without fear of writers and editors being hauled off to court or the government shutting the publication down. Russia and Venezuela could use some of that magic. It also ensures that the government can't prevent MoveOn.org, Tea Partiers or the International Brotherhood of Socialists from getting together, if they're so inclined. And it ensures that you can practice whatever religion you want to without the state getting all up in your grill.

THE SECOND AMENDMENT

An Awkward Clump of Words, Commas

A well regulated Militia, being necessary to the security of a free State, the right of the people to keep and bear Arms, shall not be infringed.

If there was one amendment that many people would like the Founding Fathers to go back and reword for clarification, this would have to be it. Depending on where you stand, the Second Amendment allows for all of us to carry handguns, fully automatic assault rifles, bazookas and hand grenades. Or it requires that we join a militia, march and start doing push-ups. It's clunky and worded in an archaic style with commas in weird places—so the end result is a battle of ideologies that has made it one of those big issues that will likely never be resolved without a civil war of some sort. It has spawned numerous catchy bumper stickers like:

- I'm NRA and I vote
- You can pry my gun from my cold, dead hands
- If guns are outlawed, only outlaws will have guns

After every campus massacre, the gun debate gets another brief moment in the spotlight before all parties acknowledge it's absolutely pointless to continue. Gun control advocates should look at the bright side: The Second Amendment, much like Dungeons & Dragons, has enabled many overweight and emasculated men to feel powerful, if not just for a brief moment.

THE THIRD AMENDMENT

Get Off My Lawn!

No Soldier shall, in time of peace be quartered in
any house, without the consent of the Owner, nor in
time of war, but in a manner to be prescribed by law.

Basically in peacetime the military can't use your house as a bar-
racks. Fair enough. And in wartime they'd need the backing of a
law and still would have to ask nicely. Some people might be more
than happy to allow soldiers to stay at their home, though some
men might fear that their daughters or wives might be led astray by
young, clean-cut, presumably horny and likely armed men in uni-
form. Knowing how much my wife likes uniforms, I'd claim to have
moldy pillows or direct them to the neighbor's larger apartment.

Perhaps a farmer with beautiful daughters might feel more comfortable quartering gay soldiers.

Regardless, if the domestic sitrep is so bad that the government
is passing laws saying troops can stay over at your place—well that's
probably the least of your troubles. Clearly you should be consider-
ing a move to Canada.

THE FOURTH AMENDMENT

Privacy, Please

The right of the people to be secure in their persons, houses, papers, and effects, against unreason-
able searches and seizures, shall not be violated, and
no Warrants shall issue, but upon probable cause,

> supported by Oath or affirmation, and particularly
> describing the place to be searched, and the persons
> or things to be seized.

Much like the First Amendment, the Fourth is regularly brushed aside when it becomes an inconvenience to something the government wants to do. This poor amendment has fallen victim to the endless War on Drugs and more recently the potentially endless War on Terror. In fact, you could well argue that it should be counted as another victim of September 11. The PATRIOT Act seized it, tossed it into the back of a sedan and drove off. Whether it's lying in a shallow grave somewhere or was simply beaten to a pulp and left for dead remains to be seen.

When you find the government rummaging through your knapsack or fondling your genitals at a TSA checkpoint, you're supposed to remind them about this amendment existing. They know it does, but they're hoping you don't, or that you're not too serious about it. And sadly, there is no shortage of people who aren't too serious about it. "What's the big deal?" they ask. "It makes us safer," they claim. Benjamin Franklin's oft-paraphrased musing applies here: "They who can give up essential liberty to obtain a little temporary safety, deserve neither liberty nor safety."

If you remind them about the Fourth Amendment loud enough the government might very well throw their hands up and walk away. But more often than not, folks fall for the old "we're doing it for your own good" line—keeping you safe by eschewing warrants and all that annoying, time-consuming "legal" stuff—and violating your rights in the process.

When the police department slaps a GPS tracking device on your car without a warrant, or seizes said car in a bust to sell for profit—they're showing little regard for this particular amendment. In September 2010 the Obama administration pushed for "backdoor" access to your communications on BlackBerry, Skype, Facebook, iChat—you name it! If George W. Bush or any Republican for that matter had proposed such sweeping, intrusive, awful Orwellian reforms, the backlash would have been furious and loud. But because the Democrats enjoy much more of a "good guy" image than the evil Republicans, the response was muted at best.

As expected, the general counsel for the FBI defended the proposal as being necessary to "protect the public safety and national security." Notwithstanding the fact that giving the government the ability to break in to your private communications opens up a whole new world of potential for abuse. And we all know that if the storied history of mission creep is any indication, those powers *will* be abused.

When a security apparatus or police force wipes their bum with Amendment IV, they always make sure you know it's *for your own good*. Much like sanitizing a condemned man's arm with an alcohol swab before his lethal injection.

THE FIFTH AMENDMENT

I'll Just Shut Up Now

No person shall be held to answer for a capital, or otherwise infamous crime, unless on a presentment or indictment of a Grand Jury, except in cases arising in the land or naval forces, or in the Militia, when in actual service in time of War or public danger; nor shall any person be subject for the same offence to be twice put in jeopardy of life or limb; nor shall be compelled in any criminal case to be a witness against himself, nor be deprived of life, liberty, or property, without due process of law; nor shall private property be taken for public use, without just compensation.

Again, another amendment popular with people who are kind of familiar with the Constitution. Most of us recognize the saying "I'm pleading the Fifth," which has been used in every legal drama ever created, and no doubt every legal drama awaiting us in the future. Anyone who lived through the Iran-Contra affair is familiar with Colonel Oliver North standing there snappily dressed and military-ish, pleading the Fifth. We understand it as allowing us to say in effect, "Hey, you all think I'm kind of guilty and I see no point in confirming your suspicions."

But there's more to the Fifth Amendment than that. In addition to the right to not incriminate yourself in court or under interrogation (lawyer up, people!), it's also the right to be properly indicted if the authorities decide they'd like you to sleep over at their place. It also states your property can't be taken without just compensation, which is nice to know. And, it forbids your being tried twice for the same crime. Good news for O. J. Simpson, bad news for the two people he was found not-guilty-in-a-criminal-trial-but-guilty-in-a-civil-trial of butchering.

THE SIXTH AMENDMENT

Try Me to the Moon

In all criminal prosecutions, the accused shall enjoy
the right to a speedy and public trial, by an impar-
tial jury of the State and district wherein the crime
shall have been committed, which district shall
have been previously ascertained by law, and to be
informed of the nature and cause of the accusation;
to be confronted with the witnesses against him; to
have compulsory process for obtaining witnesses in
his favor, and to have the Assistance of Counsel for
his defence.

The Sixth Amendment takes issue with the old-fashioned habit of
letting people rot in jail without trying them. If you've ever been ar-
rested before (I'm not judging you), you would probably appreciate
that. Sure, you're going to spend some time in jail as the police do
their paperwork, take coffee breaks, chat, call their wives and solve
crimes—but letting you languish there for a great length of time is a
violation of your constitutional rights.

Unfortunately, we're slowly getting used to the idea of letting that
happen by stretching the rules. What happens if the government
really, really wants people to waste away without trying them? They
send them to Guantánamo because that's Cuba and the U.S. Constitution doesn't apply there. *Clever!*

In addition to a speedy trial—and *speedy* is a relative term, as
anyone who's suffered through a lawsuit, contested divorce or double
homicide prosecution can tell you—you are entitled to two other

things, both important: The first is a lawyer, for one, which is great news for unemployed lawyers and those of us unfamiliar with the laws we're being prosecuted with. The second is trial by a jury of your peers. That comes much to the dismay of the thousands of people who at this very moment are suffering in outdated courthouses and posting Facebook status updates like "Crap! Stuck in Jury Duty. :-("

THE SEVENTH AMENDMENT

I'm Over Here! In the Corner!

In Suits at common law, where the value in controversy shall exceed twenty dollars, the right of trial
by jury shall be preserved, and no fact tried by a
jury, shall be otherwise re-examined in any Court
of the United States, than according to the rules of
the common law.

You don't hear much about this amendment, which entitles you to a jury trial in federal civil court cases, because there aren't many civil court cases heard in federal courts these days. If you're running for elected office, this is one of the amendments you don't have to focus on too much before a debate.

THE EIGHTH AMENDMENT

No Aye for an Eye

Excessive bail shall not be required, nor excessive
fines imposed, nor cruel and unusual punishments
inflicted.

If you find yourself sentenced to beheading in a football stadium for the crime of public drunkenness then you could rightfully be upset that your Eighth Amendment rights were being violated. Ditto if you're fined fifty-eight thousand dollars for blocking a fire hydrant. This amendment, commonly known as the "Cruel and Unusual Punishment Amendment," aims to make sure the fine fits the crime. You can't be stoned to death for having a mistress or have your hand sawed off for petty theft. That's welcome news for philanderers and kleptomaniacs, but sure to upset the sharia crowd. Then again, the things that don't upset the sharia crowd could all fit on a Post-it.

Naturally, in a world where you can have a president saying that oral sex is not considered sex, what is actually considered cruel and unusual is also up for debate. Fortunately for waterboarding enthusiasts, taking detainees to countries where we haven't yet exported our Constitution gets them around the issue yet again. Politically, anyway. Ethically it presents a few problems.

THE NINTH AMENDMENT

Know What I'm Sayin'?

> The enumeration in the Constitution, of certain rights, shall not be construed to deny or disparage others retained by the people.

Like the Second Amendment, this pithy little thing has had to suffer the slings and arrows of multiple interpretations. Perhaps it made complete sense to the Framers at the time but now it reads like a line from a Nostradamus prophecy and as a result has a different meaning depending on the whims and wishes of the reader.

Constitutional scholars and justices have talked about this amendment being everything from a pool of future rights, to a guide to how to interpret the whole document, to an inkblot.

THE TENTH AMENDMENT

Don't Mess with Texas, or Maine, or Iowa . . .

The powers not delegated to the United States by the Constitution, nor prohibited by it to the States, are reserved to the States respectively, or to the people.

In other words, the federal government should leave any powers it wasn't given under the Constitution up to the individual states. When people get cranky that the federal government is too big, too intrusive and not authorized to do X, Y or Z, this is the amendment that gets cited, and the people citing it are called Tenthers.

Different Tenthers have different goals—but they all share the same reality that beating the federal government in the governance game is an uphill battle. Current struggles include demanding state National Guard troops be returned from overseas deployment, opposition to federal drug laws, opposition to national ID cards, opposition to federal firearms laws and opposition to national health-care laws. Perhaps the most contentious debate at the moment is the one happening on the U.S.-Mexico border, with states such as Arizona passing immigration legislation that prompted the federal government to take the state to court.

The Tenth Amendment has been cropping up with more frequency over the years as citizens have started to increasingly feel that the centralized federal government has its fingers in too many pies.

THE OTHER SEVENTEEN

The ten amendments in the Bill of Rights set out to clarify things and ensure that things proceeded smoothly from that point onward. Then came the others. But not too many others. After more than 234 years of this country's existence there have only been twenty-seven amendments. The last was in 1992. That averages out to one every fourteen years (if you count the Bill of Rights as one). Amendments aren't common because they're a tremendous pain in the ass to get passed. And again, that's a good thing. That's where *It takes an act of Congress* comes from. If ratifying an amendment were easy, we'd be on Amendment CCCLVII and trying to remember which one dictated exactly what color our socks had to be.

THE ELEVENTH AMENDMENT

Chuck from Wyoming v. Missouri, et al.

> The Judicial power of the United States shall not be construed to extend to any suit in law or equity, commenced or prosecuted against one of the United States by Citizens of another State, or by Citizens or Subjects of any Foreign State.

Knowing what this amendment is about will help you greatly with pub trivia games but probably not much else. It clarifies the jurisdiction of federal courts with regard to legal actions brought against a state by a citizen of another state. In effect, it means that states don't have sovereign immunity and they can be pursued in the courts by individuals from other states.

So, if I lived in Idaho (I don't) and felt I'd been wronged by the state of California (I do) and I wanted to take them to court (can't be bothered), California could not simply say, "Nyah! Nyah! I'm California so bugger off!" That would be a terribly immature thing for California to say, anyway.

THE TWELFTH AMENDMENT

But I Digress . . .

The Electors shall meet in their respective states, and vote by ballot for President and Vice-President, one of whom, at least, shall not be an inhabitant of the same state with themselves; they shall name in their ballots the person voted for as President, and in distinct ballots the person voted for as Vice-President, and they shall make distinct lists of all persons voted for as President, and of all persons voted for as Vice-President and of the number of votes for each, which lists they shall sign and certify, and transmit sealed to the seat of the government of the United States, directed to the President of the Senate; yaddayaddayadda [TRUNCATED FOR YOUR SANITY]

The Twelfth Amendment, also known as "the First Really Long Amendment," was the first of several amendments that had a lot of words in them. So, in less than a hundred years we went from the quick and to-the-pointness of the Founders to the *lemme tell ya somethin' else* of the Blabby McBlabbersons who were apparently in Congress by that time.

One of the things this amendment does is redefine how the Electoral College works with regard to the president and vice president. The Electoral College is something people hate when their candidate wins the popular election but loses the race. Otherwise they're fine with it.

It's interesting to note that the amendment stipulates that the president and vice president cannot come from the same state. In the 2000 election a lawsuit alleged that George W. Bush and Dick Cheney were both Texans. In fact, Cheney had lived there for years, but mere months before the election he'd changed his license back to his native Wyoming and put his Dallas house up for sale. Yeah, a little shady, sure, but it's Dick Cheney, a man who can shoot you in the face and get you to apologize. The case was thrown out in appeals.

This amendment also makes sure we know that the vice president must also meet all the qualifications for being president—natural-born citizen and all that. Because it would have sucked if the vice president was from France and then the president died and *voilà*—we've got a French president.

THE THIRTEENTH AMENDMENT

You're Not the Boss of Me

1. Neither slavery nor involuntary servitude, except as a punishment for crime whereof the party

shall have been duly convicted, shall exist within
the United States, or any place subject to their
jurisdiction.
2. Congress shall have power to enforce this article
by appropriate legislation.

The Thirteenth Amendment outlawed slavery and involuntary
servitude, limiting it to the chain gangs of Arizona sheriff Joe Arpaio
and various unpaid internships. It was introduced by Republicans,
which is probably news to a lot of people.

This was the final nail in the coffin of the trade in humans. Of
course, the racism thing lingered a bit.

Having been fully emancipated, negroes were free to insist you
stop calling them negroes. Emancipated coloreds soon asked that
you stop calling them that too. Emancipated blacks said that actually they'd prefer being called African-Americans after all, and finally
all was well with the world. Unless you were being called African-
American but were actually from the Caribbean, in which case you
wanted to be called Caribbean-American or black. Or, if you were
actor Avery Brooks you called yourself brown—just to complicate
things even more. But eventually black people decided that being
called black wasn't so bad after all, and they told white people you
could call them black, and white people and black people weren't
quite sure who or what had a problem with the word in the first
place. Much like the word *stewardess.*

THE FOURTEENTH AMENDMENT

Here's How It's Gonna Be, See?

1. All persons born or naturalized in the United
   States, and subject to the jurisdiction thereof,
   are citizens of the United States and of the State
   wherein they reside. No State shall make or enforce any law which shall abridge the privileges
   or immunities of citizens of the United States;
   nor shall any State deprive any person of life,
   liberty, or property, without due process of law;
   nor deny to any person within its jurisdiction
   the equal protection of the laws. Yaddayaddayadda. [AGAIN, TRUNCATED TO SPARE
   YOU]

This pot-luck amendment continued the unfortunate new trend
of amendments blabbering like an alcoholic on the stool next to
you. What happened to the good old days of compact, less caloric
amendments? Remember those?

Fourteen covered several things at once: It had to spank the
Confederacy for being naughty, of course, and wanted to make sure
rebellious Confederate states would have to pay their own debts. It
also made sure that any legislators who'd been on the wrong side of
the Civil War—you know, the ones who call it "the War of North-
ern Aggression"—would now ensure their allegiance to the United
States.

It effectively overruled *Dred Scott* and stipulated that citizens
enjoyed federal and state rights. Even black ones! Yes, technically

everyone was equal under the law. It was a novel idea at the time. It dealt with due process and citizenship issues.

And it instructed that all residents of a state would be counted when determining the number of representatives, overriding the Constitution's original "3/5 compromise" that counted only 3/5 of a state's slave population. Great news for people who hate fractions.

THE FIFTEENTH AMENDMENT

Rock the Vote

1. The right of citizens of the United States to vote shall not be denied or abridged by the United States or by any State on account of race, color, or previous condition of servitude.
2. The Congress shall have the power to enforce this article by appropriate legislation.

Simply put, any eligible citizen of the United States may vote, regardless of race, color or creed. Contrary to popular belief there's absolutely nothing in here that dictates that a black person can only vote for a black candidate.

Hear that sound? That's the roar of hundreds of thousands of men cheering their newfound rights! Just men, of course. You'll still need to be sporting a penis if you want to get into the polls. Sorry, ladies!

THE SIXTEENTH AMENDMENT

Booooooooooooooooooooooooooooooooooo!

The Congress shall have power to lay and collect
taxes on incomes, from whatever source derived,
without apportionment among the several States,
and without regard to any census or enumeration.

To their credit, Rhode Island, Connecticut and Utah said no.
And Virginia, Florida and Pennsylvania just turned their backs and
pretended it didn't exist. But Sixteen was ratified in 1913 and that
very same year the beloved Form 1040 was born. It was only four
pages long and possibly took you twenty minutes to complete if you
were a slow writer or your quill was worn out.

Nearly a century later, Form 1040 is just a little-bitty piece of a
wholly incomprehensible and absurd tax code that would wipe out
a forest if you printed it out. Those of us not affiliated with H&R
Block spend the first four months of every year cursing the dreaded
thing—hoarding scraps of paper, itemizing, calculating deprecia-
tion, deducting, tracking how many miles we put on our SUVs last
week and blaming all the inevitable mistakes on TurboTax.

Meanwhile, politicians like New York congressman Charlie Rangel seem unfazed by it all.

THE SEVENTEENTH AMENDMENT

Release the Kraken!

The Senate of the United States shall be composed of two Senators from each State, elected by the people thereof, for six years; and each Senator shall have one vote. The electors in each State shall have the qualifications requisite for electors of the most numerous branch of the State legislatures.

When vacancies happen in the representation of any State in the Senate, the executive authority of such State shall issue writs of election to fill such vacancies: Provided, That the legislature of any State may empower the executive thereof to make temporary appointments until the people fill the vacancies by election as the legislature may direct.

This amendment shall not be so construed as to affect the election or term of any Senator chosen before it becomes valid as part of the Constitution.

Originally the election of senators was up to state legislatures, not ordinary people like us. There was logic to this: The senator could focus on doing his job rather than wasting his time trying to get elected. It would also mean the senator would be more in tune with his state's government and legislators because he would have to kiss their collective bums. Not to mention, conventional wisdom was that the masses were a little too uninformed to be tasked with such an important decision as choosing a senator.

But times changed, and a movement ensued to take the power

away from the state legislatures and give it to the people. With the Seventeenth Amendment they finally succeeded. Those of us familiar with terribly corrupt and dysfunctional state legislatures like New York's should be able to understand.

You're probably thinking *sure, okay, whatever* but Seventeen crops up every now and then. In the 2010 midterm elections, Alaska Tea Party candidate Joe Miller made waves when he proposed abolishing the amendment. Critics, and the other candidates, quickly admonished him for wanting to "take the vote away from the people." But he may have had a point, because when the people are willing to consider electing someone like embarrassing Delaware candidate Christine O'Donnell, maybe letting a state legislature decide isn't so bad after all.

Anyway, the odds of a repeal happening now are pretty slim, seeing as folks in the Senate are now quite comfortable with the way things work. They know exactly the special interests they're selling themselves to, and understand the voter base that they have to pander to—so making them start from scratch really seems unfair. To them, anyway.

THE EIGHTEENTH AMENDMENT

How Dry We Am

1. After one year from the ratification of this article the manufacture, sale, or transportation of intoxicating liquors within, the importation thereof into, or the exportation thereof from the United States and all territory subject to the jurisdiction thereof for beverage purposes is hereby prohibited.

2. The Congress and the several States shall have concurrent power to enforce this article by appropriate legislation.

3. This article shall be inoperative unless it shall have been ratified as an amendment to the Constitution by the legislatures of the several States, as provided in the Constitution, within seven years from the date of the submission hereof to the States by the Congress.

Bastards. You'd think that getting both houses of Congress to approve Prohibition would have been difficult, given that there was likely no shortage of drunks on either side of the aisle in both the House and Senate—but apparently it wasn't that hard. Despite the framework set by the Founding Fathers, a bunch of proselytizing teetotaler busybodies managed to overcome the odds and get this sucker through, forcing their self-declared morals and virtues on an entire country by prohibiting the manufacture and sale of alcohol in the United States. Bastards.

In this dreadful amendment we have a shining example of the Law of Unintended Consequences: when what you wanted to happen and what actually happens wind up being two very different things.

Presumably, through the good grace of this amendment, America was to have become a sober utopia of incredibly productive citizens. No longer tempted by the lure of drink, we'd have ample time to admire our wives, play with our kids, study our Bibles and manicure the lawn. An end to crime! And end to poverty! An end to alcoholism!

In the end, this amendment accomplished nothing of the sort. In fact, it proved beyond a doubt that people like their vices. A lot.

And the appeal of that sin was too much to handle. We drank gin made in bathtubs. We went blind from moonshine. We worked out secret knocks to gain entrance to speakeasies. And since it was all illegal anyway, the drinking age didn't exist.

This amendment put taxpaying bars out of business and made nontaxpaying psychopaths like Al Capone rich and infamous. Scores died from unregulated booze. Hordes of gangsters and law enforcement officers were gunned down in mafia turf wars. (Valentine's Day massacre, anyone?) And everyone kept drinking—even if it was officially illegal. To quote H. L. Mencken:

"Not only are crime, poverty and disease undiminished, but drunkenness itself, if the police statistics are to be believed, has greatly increased. The land rocks with the scandal. Prohibition has made the use of alcohol devilish and even fashionable, and so vastly augmented the number of users. The young of both sexes, mainly innocent of the cup under license, now take to it almost unanimously. In brief, Prohibition has not only failed to work the benefits that its proponents promised in 1917; it has brought in so many new evils that even the mob has turned against it."

As they say in politics: Mission accomplished!

THE NINETEENTH AMENDMENT

Yes, She Can!

The right of citizens of the United States to vote shall not be denied or abridged by the United States or by any State on account of sex.

Congress shall have power to enforce this article by appropriate legislation.

With this amendment, women finally had the right to cancel out their husband's vote.

THE TWENTIETH AMENDMENT

Details, Details

1. The terms of the President and Vice President shall end at noon on the 20th day of January, and the terms of Senators and Representatives at noon on the 3d day of January, of the years in which such terms would have ended if this article had not been ratified; and the terms of their successors shall then begin. Yaddayaddayadda. [TRUNCATED OUT OF DEFERENCE TO COMMON DECENCY]

This clunker establishes protocol in the event a president dies of excitement after getting elected but before he is sworn in. The most important part of this amendment stipulates that the new president officially takes office at noon on January 20.

It goes without saying that the new president will be sporting gray hair within four months of this date.

THE TWENTY-FIRST AMENDMENT

Our Bad! Cheers!

1. The eighteenth article of amendment to the Constitution of the United States is hereby repealed.

The Twenty-First Amendment acknowledges that, yes, we are in fact a nation of freedom-loving drunks and that a blanket prohibition of alcohol was very dumb indeed. Screw you, teetotalers! Finally, America was free to go on a pub crawl and brew embarrassingly bad beers like Budweiser.

It serves as testament to the ability of Congress to unite to correct a wrong—especially one that directly affects them. You can rest assured that this amendment was passed because 90 percent of our congressmen were tired of smuggling bottles of Canadian whiskey into their offices.

Just because the War on Booze failed miserably and prompted this amendment does not in any way mean we actually learned any kind of lesson from it. That would be ridiculous! By the time the War on Drugs got going some decades later, this particular moment in history had been long forgotten.

THE TWENTY-SECOND AMENDMENT

Enough Already

1. No person shall be elected to the office of the President more than twice, and no person who has held the office of President, or acted as President, for more than two years of a term to which some other person was elected President shall be elected to the office of the President more than once. But this Article shall not apply to any person holding the office of President when this Article was proposed by the Congress, and shall not prevent any person who may be holding the office of President, or acting as President, during

the term within which this Article becomes operative from holding the office of President or acting as President during the remainder of such term.

2. This article shall be inoperative unless it shall have been ratified as an amendment to the Constitution by the legislatures of three-fourths of the several States within seven years from the date of its submission to the States by the Congress.

Also known as the "Franklin Delano Roosevelt Was President Too Long Amendment," this limits a president to two terms. Too much of a good thing, as they say. Or too much of a bad thing, as the other side would say.

For the better part of the country's existence, presidents refrained from seeking a third term—even though they could have. FDR had three, won a fourth, but died shortly afterward.

Jimmy Carter and George H. W. Bush, both defeated after only one term, are eligible to run again—which is great news for Jimmy Carter and George H. W. Bush.

THE TWENTY-THIRD AMENDMENT

I See D.C.

1. The District constituting the seat of Government of the United States shall appoint in such manner as the Congress may direct: A number of electors of President and Vice President equal

to the whole number of Senators and Representatives in Congress to which the District would be entitled if it were a State, but in no event more than the least populous State; they shall be in addition to those appointed by the States, but they shall be considered, for the purposes of the election of President and Vice President, to be electors appointed by a State; and they shall meet in the District and perform such duties as provided by the twelfth article of amendment.

2. The Congress shall have power to enforce this article by appropriate legislation.

This boring amendment details the selection of electors for Washington, D.C., and lets the good citizens of the district actually have the right to vote. Feel free to scream "You're violating my Twenty-Third Amendment rights!" the next time you get a speeding ticket, and see if the cop lets you off. Always worth a try.

THE TWENTY-FOURTH AMENDMENT

Rocking the Vote Now Free

1. The right of citizens of the United States to vote in any primary or other election for President or Vice President, for electors for President or Vice President, or for Senator or Representative in Congress, shall not be denied or abridged by the United States or any State by reason of failure to pay any poll tax or other tax.

2. The Congress shall have power to enforce this article by appropriate legislation.

The Fifteenth Amendment allowed anyone to vote regardless of race, color or creed. That bugged certain folks, so some creative but naughty southern states (we won't name names) tried to do an end-run around Fifteen by charging money to vote—a poll tax. The tax could be waived if your ancestors had voted prior to the abolition of slavery, which would have meant they were white. Which would have meant that you were too. Which meant that this tax was specifically designed to apply to blacks and Native Americans.

The logic was pretty simple: *Most black people are poor, therefore most black people won't be able to vote! Hee-hee!*

This amendment killed the poll tax and effectively shut off that avenue of discrimination, forcing some people to devise other ways of preventing people they don't want to vote from voting. Like intimidating them, or hiding the voter registration office.

THE TWENTY-FIFTH AMENDMENT

Successories

1. In case of the removal of the President from office or of his death or resignation, the Vice President shall become President.
2. Whenever there is a vacancy in the office of the Vice President, the President shall nominate a Vice President who shall take office upon confirmation by a majority vote of both Houses of

Congress. Yaddayaddayadda. [TRUNCATED
FOR BORINGNESS]

This details the succession of the office of the presidency in the
event the president dies or is incapacitated while in office. It has
been incorporated into the stories of many disaster movies and was
apparently unknown to Alexander "I'm in Charge Now!" Haig after
the shooting of President Ronald Reagan in 1981. Had he read up
on his Twenty-Fifth Amendment, he'd have known that George
H. W. Bush was next in line in the event Reagan died. Of course,
Reagan didn't die. Thirty years later he's fondly remembered as the
Greatest President in the History of Ever by conservatives traumatized by George W. Bush's unique interpretation of conservatism.

The succession of the presidency became a significant factor in the
2008 election when voters looked at John McCain and realized he
would be 72.3942 years old when he assumed the presidency. If he were
to die, that would have made Vice President Sarah Palin the president.

Then, assuming that Palin would quit halfway through her term,
as she was wont to do, Speaker of the House Nancy Pelosi would
become the president—and those were two risks voters were unwilling to take.

THE TWENTY-SIXTH AMENDMENT

The Right for the MTV Generation to Ruin Everything

1. The right of citizens of the United States, who
   are eighteen years of age or older, to vote shall
   not be denied or abridged by the United States
   or by any State on account of age.

2. The Congress shall have power to enforce this
article by appropriate legislation.

Imagine you're eighteen and some miserable old coot running for office says that it's perfectly okay for you to be drafted and sent off to an unpopular war. Problem is, the voting age is twenty-one so you're not able to go to the polls to tell that miserable old coot just how you feel about his law.

This amendment fixes that. They figured if you can be called up to go fight and die in a war you don't want to be in, you should probably have the right to influence the politicians who would be making those kinds of decisions. Can't really argue with that. Plus, you get a bonus: Anyone who remembers their youth knows that eighteen-year-olds have all the answers.

Frankly, it seems kind of unfair that an eighteen-year-old can fight and die in a war but still has to wait three years to buy a lousy, overly sweet wine cooler.

THE TWENTY-SEVENTH AMENDMENT

Show Me the Money, but Not Right Now

No law, varying the compensation for the services
of the Senators and Representatives, shall take effect, until an election of representatives shall have
intervened.

Only 202 years in the making! That's right—the idea behind Twenty-Seven came from 1789. But when it comes to Congress policing Congress—those things take time. This amendment prevents

Congress from voting itself an instant pay raise. Yup, they're going to have to wait until the *next* term for it to take effect. Not much of a sacrifice, sure, and it took two centuries, but it's Congress. What did you expect? Something quick and significant?

THE LAW OF THE LAND

And there you have it: a four-page document and twenty-seven follow-up amendments that serve as the basic framework of the world's longest-lasting democracy. And by democracy, we mean constitutional republic.

5

THE U.S. GOVERNMENT

Building an empire with a few branches
and a lot of checks

Talk to anyone with a third-grade or higher education about the U.S. government and they'll likely mutter something about checks and balances. We may not know much, but we know about checks and balances and when you get an American going about his government you are damn well going to hear about them. It's all "checks and balances" this and "checks and balances" that. Maybe we're not all too sure what exactly those checks and balances actually do, or if they even work, but we know they're there somewhere and besides—it's the thought that counts, as I tell my wife every time she's disappointed by a present.

The Founding Fathers were really big on those checks and balances because they were emotionally scarred by King George III's arbitrary, authoritarian rule. They really didn't like one guy calling all the shots. It occurred to them when founding their new government (as founders do) that too much power in any one person's hands is always a terrible, terrible thing. We've seen it with world leaders throughout history.

And we've certainly seen it with Oprah.

Desperate to have a government that wasn't just creating another pseudo-monarch or other cocky, all-powerful type calling the shots, these men set about establishing the checking and balancing of power, hoping to deprive any one power-hungry jackass from eventually having all of it. They knew darn well that there's always a power-hungry jackass waiting in the wings for his moment to seize control and fire up a brand-new dictatorship. And though Harry S. Truman once said dictatorship was the most efficient kind of government, and it probably is, it's never the most enjoyable, as evidenced by the various depressing-ocracies in North Korea, Venezuela, Saudi Arabia, Syria, Belarus and Turkmenistan, to name only a few.

No, our founding lads wanted a happy and free nation with power diluted via distribution. And not just distribution to anyone, mind you, but distribution with some modicum of quality control. They knew that a direct democracy, one with every Tom, Dick and Harry voting on national policy, would be nothing short of disastrous. Sure, we'll hear Joe the Plumber's opinion on things, but no one in their right mind wants him voting on international treaties, energy bills or trade legislation, do they? If you disagree, just wander around Disney World for ten minutes and imagine all those folks having direct say in all matters.

The Founders wanted a government with powers distributed among esteemed individuals who were smarter and savvier than the masses they would be representing. Fortunately for the Founders, that turned out to be people just like them!

They created three branches of government, all with different powers, all forced to work together in varying degrees. To compromise. To negotiate. To divide the pie equitably and fairly. No longer would one person with a stupid idea be able to steamroll his stupid idea into a legal reality. No, he would be forced to first sell his stupid idea to his legislative colleagues, convincing them that his stupid idea wasn't so stupid after all. And if Congress gave the thumbs-up to his stupid idea, he would once again have to convince the chief executive to not veto his stupid idea. And assuming he got that far, he'd still have to hope that his stupid idea wasn't so stupid as to be called unconstitutional by the robed and serious folks over at the judicial branch.

So sure, you can accomplish a lot of stupid things, but you really have to work at it. And it's time consuming. The system that's in place is the equivalent of those annoying speed bumps they put down in residential areas. You have no choice but to plod along slowly, muttering and cursing the whole way until you get to where you were hoping to go.

So hooray for checks and balances.

That's not to say people haven't tried to uncheck and unbalance the system over the course of history. There's always some sort of mischief going on, always some politician somewhere with grand ideas, devoting his time and energy to outwitting the system. Fortunately for us, it's a frustrating experience for them that quite often has them throwing their hands up like someone who lost a quarter to a vending machine. It's not a perfect system but it's a damn good system if you look at all the various, predominantly lousy and regrettable systems of government the world has managed to come up with.

Here is what we've got:

THE LEGISLATIVE BRANCH

The legislative branch is composed of the House of Representatives and the Senate. They have better health care than you do.

Being in Congress is increasingly attractive because it allows you to enjoy all the perks of power without any of the annoyances of accountability so commonly found in the private sector. Forty years ago you could run for public office for the price of a high-end Mercedes. Alas, demand is high now and getting in is no longer cheap. Today, if you manage to spend a million dollars for the House or several million for the Senate you're getting off real easy. Even adjusted for inflation those numbers are totally nuts.

Congress handles pretty much anything to do with money—from the taking of it to the spending of it. Unlike a normal business, if they spend too much of it there aren't many repercussions—they simply turn to you and ask for more! Unfortunately, like a coed with a spiked drink, most of us lack the resources or wherewithal to resist their advances.

Congress is responsible for budgetary matters, which involves their grabbing the best-sounding number out of thin air and then shrugging their shoulders when that number eventually proves to have been absurdly optimistic. They're responsible for providing for the country's defense and the welfare of the American people. That's probably why you're going, "Uh oh" right about now.

But wait, there's more!

Congress holds domain over the postal service, road systems, patents and copyrights and establishing standards for weights and measures. It was Congress that talked about "going metric" back in the 1970s, but they never got around to it. Too bad, because going 88 kph sounds much cooler than 55 mph.

Congress has power to oversee the executive branch, including the power to impeach and remove the president or other naughty federal functionaries. They can also send you as much mail as they please, at no cost to them, as long as said mail is not considered "election materials." Naturally that definition gets pushed to the limit as you approach an election.

The role of Congress with regard to our national defense includes their *exclusive* ability to declare war. Yes, the italics are there to emphasize absurdity, because many of us know that declaring war *used* to be Congress's exclusive right. Teddy Roosevelt didn't bother asking when he sent the military to Panama. Truman and Johnson took the Orwellian route: tired of asking for permission to have a war, they simply called them "police actions" and pushed the GO button. The Obama administration called it a "Kinetic Military Action"! Semantics rule! You see, it all really depends on what your definition of *war* is.

The number of representatives each state has is based on the state's population. Each state's population is based on the census, the decennial head count that has talk show hosts foaming at the mouth and conspiracy theorists diving behind the sofa whenever some underpaid census underling rings the doorbell to ask how many toilets they have. Since we had a census in 2010, we'll have an approximate head count for the country. More population means more districts and that means more seats in the House. The current 435 House seats will likely be increased by the time we get to the 2012 election, so start collecting craploads of money and staking out positions, congressional hopefuls!

Each state gets two senators regardless of the state's size. So even if it's puny Rhode Island or gargantuan California—two senators. Probably a good thing because that's already a lot of ego for one state to handle.

Having a bicameral (two-chamber) Congress wasn't the original idea. Heavier-populated states wanted to have congressional representation based on population. That would ultimately have been swell for population juggernauts New York, Texas and California, whose scores of representatives would have wound up making all the rules for the rest of us. But that's a terrifying prospect if you've ever spent time in New York, Texas or California. The delicately populated states like North Dakota, Rhode Island and Montana would have been rendered helpless—with their one or two delegates easily tackled and beaten to death by the others.

Naturally the little guys liked the two-representatives-per-state model. That way the big states wouldn't be the boss of everybody else and all states would have equal say in federal affairs. But that wasn't necessarily ideal either, because bigger states have bigger problems that might be too much for just two little senators to handle.

Like someone who can't decide between steak or lobster, the Founders opted to just go ahead and have both. A bicameral legislature. Two houses. One for Economy class, the other for Platinum Medallion. They called it "the Great Compromise," which, coincidentally, is also what they call the marriage of gorgeous young models to bloated old billionaires.

OUR HOUSE OF COMMONS

In addition to all the things they do as federal lawmakers, those elected to the House of Representatives have to deal with the unwashed masses, the rabble, the commoner. That'd be you and me. It's their job to keep in touch with their constituents—to *represent* them if you will—and to work on localized issues and legislation of particular importance to the people in their (gerrymandered)

district. In that sense they're more "hands-on" with their constituents. And by that I don't mean groping, except in some cases.

One of the reasons congressmen serve only a two-year term is that the Founders wanted them to remember who they were working for back home. *Clever.* The short term has its downsides though—one congresswoman told me that unless you're well established and your congressional seat totally safe, you ultimately spend one year working on legislation and one year fund-raising to stay in office. She didn't like that so she ran for Senate instead, and lost terribly.

OUR HOUSE OF LORDS

By virtue of the two-per-state mandate, the Senate is an intimate gathering of power players. You could easily fit all of them into just two cars on our heavily subsidized, inefficient, money-hemorrhaging national train system.

Senators are less accessible to you and me because they don't represent districts, they represent entire states. To use a T.G.I. Friday's analogy: Representatives are like the managers of an individual T.G.I. Friday's. They deal directly with their employees and the store's customers who come to them with all their problems: "I need next Tuesday off" or "My fajitas are cold." Senators, then, are like the district managers. They represent a large swath of T.G.I. Friday's. They deal more with higher-level problems like "We need to get the hell out of Detroit."

As if to emphasize their classism (to use a term from an old college professor) the Senate is sometimes referred to as the *Upper House* as opposed to the *Lower House,* occupied by those peasant representatives.

Before 1913, when we didn't get to vote for senators, they were elected by state legislatures. There was a logic to this because it ensured that the Senate would only consist of seasoned (i.e., elite, connected, entrenched) politicians chosen by other politicians. One could argue that this arrangement might lend itself to backroom dealings, diminished representation and corruption of a "good ol' boys" environment. And no one would be surprised if it did.

But the Seventeenth Amendment changed all that and gave the right to elect senators to the masses. That effectively allowed anyone, good ol' boy or no, connected or no, to run for a Senate seat. And that, friends, gave us many spectacles. Not the least of which would be Wicca-dabbling, masturbation-hating, science-not-knowing, debt-evading Delaware candidate Christine O'Donnell giving it her best shot, to the amusement of many.

Things move slower in the Senate—and not just because senators tend to be older and fatter. They have the luxury of time that representatives do not. Their six-year terms allow them to relax a little, and to spend much more time wheeling and dealing and inserting absurd pork projects into bills.

Senators are powerful people, and powerful people often make powerful connections. Those powerful connections often come in handy when the senator eventually enters the private sector and is looking for a cushy job from a company he gave tax breaks to when he was in office.

THE EXECUTIVE BRANCH

The executive branch is, you guessed it, the domain of the chief executive: the president of the United States. Our country's answer to Dear Leader. Did you know that at one time the presidency was a largely humble position? It's true! Particularly during peacetime the presidency was like the nation's HR department—overseeing the hiring of officials for various offices and making sure the governmental machine plodded along. Sure, it was still a sweet gig, but for quite some time the presidency was fairly uneventful and left behind a string of presidents who, like Millard Fillmore, aren't known for doing much of anything in comparison to today's globally famous, supermighty presidential titans. Can you imagine? Do you wish you could? Me too.

Alas, the laid-backness of the executive office didn't sit well with President Andrew Jackson, who, like Kanye West, really didn't like feeling upstaged. ("Yo Congress. I'm really happy for you. I'ma let you finish but . . .") He was one of the first of a long line of presidents who, like David Lee Roth, had a very good thing going but wanted more and so broke up the band.

The president is commander-in-chief of the Army, Navy, Air Force and Marine Corps. Oh, and Coast Guard I suppose.

It's also his job to handle matters of diplomacy—such as verbally spanking kooks like Ahmadinejad, Qaddafi or Kim Jong Il, kissing the bottoms of insidious Saudi royalty or giving the ancient queen of England an iPod she'll never use. It's also his job to reward his bigger campaign contributors with tasty appointments and sweet ambassadorships, to strategically choose Supreme Court justices and to fill any of the gajillion cabinet positions that exist within the behemoth of an administration we now have.

During wartime or whenever something terrible happens, nervous citizens gaze worriedly in the direction of the president and give him a what-are-you-gonna-do? look. Because of this, the role of the presidency tends to greatly expand during these national emergencies. This has not gone unnoticed. The Civil War allowed Abraham Lincoln to suspend a few liberties here and there, bend a few rules and even declare martial law that he didn't have the power to declare. That set the stage for future presidents to not let an emergency go to waste, to paraphrase former Obama administration staffer Rahm Emanuel. I'm not blaming Lincoln for the PATRIOT Act, but he's a president who set a precedent. By the time Franklin Delano Roosevelt was through with it, the presidency had been sufficiently transformed from ninety-pound weakling to hulking, semipsychopathic bully.

Nowadays, as head of the most powerful military in the world and trailed by someone holding the nuclear "football," the president is arguably the most powerful person on earth. With that tremendous power comes premature graying, as we've seen with every president in recent memory. It probably also makes you a little bit cocky.

In addition to the ability to vaporize countries, seduce interns, tap phone lines, pick bomb targets and illicitly fund rebels, the president's responsibilities include:

HEAD OF STATE: Like it or not, your president is the figurehead who represents the country here and abroad. Whether he's mispronouncing words as he stumbles through a long-winded speech, hopelessly striving for peace in the Middle East or declaring that he's a *Berliner,* all eyes are on him. He gets burned in effigy by Pakistani street mobs, has shoes thrown at him during speeches, is the butt of late-night TV jokes (if he's Republican) or appears on late-night TV (if he's a Democrat). He cordially greets opportunistic attention-hounds who sneak into White House dinners, and throws up on the Japanese prime minister when necessary.

THE STATE OF THE UNION: What once began as a very casual affair, as in a letter simply handed to Congress, is now the government's answer to the Oscars. Every year the State of the Union address provides the president with a chance to cancel all other television options and bullshit his way, for about a thousand minutes, through all the awesome things he's done and plans on doing. There's no shortage of grandstanding, posturing and blame-shifting and in all honesty the speech should be called the Here's What I Want to Do and It's Gonna Cost Ya address. It's a given that during the speech he will point to someone sitting in the audience and acknowledge their great accomplishment. The accomplishment is usually being someone who overcame an obstacle thanks to the party in power or who is related to someone who died during an act of heroism. A lot of time (and good TV show watching) could be saved if we'd just acknowledge that the president's party will agree, stand up and clap about everything he says, and the party not in power will disagree, remain seated with folded arms and frown. In a 2010 decision, Supreme Court justice Samuel Alito agreed with the previous decision of Justices Scalia and Thomas in deciding that the address was well worth not attending.

The partisan dynamic of the 2011 State of the Union address was greatly affected by the "mixed seating" arrangement that followed the Tucson shooting spree and attempted assassination of Representative Gabrielle Giffords. Although a nice gesture, it was still an awkward one. Seeing so many uncomfortable politicians in one room was kind of priceless, though.

GUY WHO SIGNS THINGS: Treaties, executive orders, laws, you name it—the president has a pen and he's not afraid to use it. Whether he's signing into law a "big fucking deal," as Joe Biden put it, or an emergency "supplemental" appropriation that funds a war outside the actual budget for that war, signing things is important. And it doesn't matter what the tab might ultimately come out to be, because just like a lobbyist with an expense account, he's not footing the bill. You are.

GRANT CLEMENCY: The president has the ability to issue pardons, commutations and remission of fines. This power has historically been used to right a wrong or show forgiveness, such as when President Jimmy Carter pardoned individuals who had evaded the draft during Vietnam. In 1974 incoming president Gerald Ford caught a lot of flak for absolving Richard Nixon of all his presidential sins. The pardon officially let Tricky Dick completely off the hook—at the small cost of Ford not getting a second term. Clemency can't be challenged, which comes in very handy especially if, like President Bill Clinton, you want to pardon some particularly shady people. Clinton's 396 pardons fall short of Truman's 1,913 or Nixon's 863, but contain enough gems that *Pardongate* entered the vernacular.

PARTY LEADER: The president serves as the party's leader, crafting the party's platform and nominating the head of his party's political committee. He also offers his services by fund-raising—enthusiastically offering up the White House Lincoln Bedroom in return for cash, for example. Popular presidents are often enlisted to campaign for candidates—jetting around to speak at dinners, rile up crowds and rally the troops. Unpopular presidents are often asked to not jet around or speak at dinners or rally the troops. As the face of the party in power, he's often expected to appear on TV as much as possible. Especially before elections when it looks like his party is about to suffer major humiliation.

VETO POWER: With one little stroke of his pen the president can smite a law in its infancy. A mere second's worth of wrist movement can trash the efforts of countless congressmen, pages, interns, lobbyists, wonks, hacks, think tanks and special interest groups, which, of course, is a pretty good thing. The threat of a veto forces Congress to tread carefully—tempering their proposed legislation and making concessions, as much as they hate to do that.

Supposedly, Congress represents the will of the people (stop laughing) so presidents tend to exercise their veto privilege carefully so as not to upset the general population. That is, except for FDR, who vetoed more than six hundred bills during his thirteen-year reign as King of America. FDR was undoubtedly empowered by a heavily Democratic Congress and the fact that Americans were far more terrified of the Depression, Nazis, Japanese and the looming Soviet threat than they were his mighty veto pen. His exuberance with killing bills would have earned him the moniker Don "Veto" Corleone if *The Godfather* had existed. Sadly, it didn't and a great pun never happened.

PILLAR OF STRENGTH: At times of trouble, the president serves to allay our fears and soothe our frayed nerves. Like whiskey. Abraham Lincoln's Gettysburg Address is an excellent example of a president stepping up, giving us a big ol' national hug and telling us everything is going to be all right. Pillar-of-strength moments usually come at those moments things are so bad that partisanship falls by the wayside: LBJ assuming JFK's shattered presidency, Ronald Reagan after the Lockerbie incident, Bill Clinton at the Oklahoma City bombing, and of course the most recent example: George W. Bush's sermon on the mount of rubble at Ground Zero. For one brief, mournful moment, traumatized Americans dropped all the "stolen election" rhetoric they'd been seething over for nearly a year and united solely as Americans, finding solace in his declaration that we'd get the bastards responsible for the atrocity.

It didn't take too long for him to squander that feeling and eventually have most of America breathing a collective sigh of relief when he went back to Crawford, but it was real nice while it lasted.

Were a comet to level an American city and bring untold death and destruction, you can rest assured that President Obama would undoubtedly address the country, soothe us with his eloquent words and make years of bitter rhetoric all but a memory. The O'Reillys, the Becks, the Levins, Breitbarts and Savages would hold hands with the Olbermanns, the Maddows, the Behars and Matthewses. They would nod their heads in agreement, reflect, shed tears and unite under the banner of being American.

Then a week or two later some schmuck with a misspelled sign would demand to see Obama's birth certificate again.

JUDICIAL BRANCH

The judicial branch includes the Supreme Court of the United States (SCOTUS), which serves as the very last word in the law of the land. It's the governmental equivalent of "Go ask your mother."

Congress and the president spar and wrangle over new legislation while the judicial branch sits quietly on the sidelines. They don't participate in the making of laws, just their enforcement. The cases that eventually make their way to the Supremes are usually of great consequence to the American people: abortion, campaign finance, gun rights, eminent domain. It's the Super Bowl of courts and for many legal practitioners, barring sleazeball personal-injury attorneys, the chance to stand before the justices and argue a case is a dream on par with winning a Pulitzer, getting drafted by the Yankees or sleeping with the Olsen twins.

If you think it's exciting for legal eagles to stand in front of the justices and match wits—imagine what it's like to actually become one. Despite FDR's best efforts to have fifteen, there are only nine justices. Landing one of those slots is statistically nearly impossible. Should you defy the odds you'll find yourself in possession of one of the sweetest of gigs on the planet because, just like unionized teachers, it's well nigh impossible to get rid of them. They're in for life—or until they've decided they've had enough—so as to prevent them from being subject to any kind of retribution by a mean-spirited president or vengeful sort.

Most presidents who serve at least one term eventually have the opportunity to appoint a justice to the High Court. The only modern one who did not have the opportunity was Jimmy Carter. Let's all breathe a collective sigh of relief.

Currently on the court you'll find two Reagan appointees, one Bush the Elder appointee, two Bush the Younger appointees, two Clinton appointees and two Obama appointees.

Ironically, one of the few places in America where we're not celebrating the bejeezus out of diversity is on the Supreme Court—all have Ivy League backgrounds and six hail from New York or New Jersey. While it may lack collegiate and geographic diversity, it is diverse ethnically, religiously and especially in the diversity of attitude toward portraiture. The two most recent justices, Kagan and Sotomayor, have chosen broad smiles that are too friendly and in direct contrast with Ginsburg's terrifying stare. Alito's sly smile is a bit disconcerting, while Breyer and Kennedy seem like cheerful grandparents. Scalia looks like he's about to unload a barrage of obscenity on you and Thomas totally looks like he's sentencing you to death. Roberts has a respectable, toothless smile that suggests the right amount of gravitas and humanity. That's probably why he's the chief justice.

HOW TO BECOME A SUPREME

To get on the Supreme Court is a Herculean task. First of all, for them to even be looking to hire requires that one of the nine slots be made available. That only happens in the event that the gods smite one, convince her to retire or get him impeached.

Assuming there's a vacancy, you now have to catch the eye of the president, because it is he who is in charge of appointing you. Making a president aware of your existence is no small task, as anyone who has wasted their time emailing the void at president@whitehouse.gov probably knows. Getting nominated definitely requires that you be of the same political persuasion as the appointing president and usually requires traveling in the same circles.

Now, if a spot opens up and the president knows you exist and likes how you think, you're certainly on the right track, but there is another fairly enormous obstacle standing between you and a black robe. There was a time when it was believed that a justice would rule impartially and objectively on laws—as judges are supposed to do in a perfect world. Believe it or not, in the past justices were approved by near majorities in the Senate. Reagan's Bork nomination may have been shot out of the sky, but appointees Scalia and Kennedy enjoyed confirmation tallies of 98–0 and 97–0, respectively. Bush the Elder's Clarence Thomas suffered the indignity of the terribly close vote of 52–48 largely due not to the color of his skin, one hopes, but rather to allegations regarding the content of his character. Clinton appointees Ginsburg and Breyer restored the spirit of bipartisan harmony with their respective 96–3 and 87–9 confirmation tallies. And then came Bush the Younger and Obama and the notion of unanimous consent went out the window. The descent began with Roberts and his 78–22 vote, followed by Alito, who squeaked by with 58–42. Obama's Sotomayor and Kagan picks netted 68–31 and 63–37, respectively.

The assumption has now become that a justice will act as political activist first and objective overseer second. Naturally, that means that confirmation hearings have become political theater at its finest. Outcomes are predetermined, yea or nay votes almost assuredly matching the number of Republicans and Democrats in the Senate.

Now, you would think that the fear of a contentious and bitter confirmation hearing would steer a president toward nominating a centrist who could calm the nerves of the opposition party enough that he or she could win over enough hearts and minds to breeze through.

But this is politics, and you'd be wrong.

The president must now announce his picks as having the right stuff, without telling you what that stuff is. Nominees must subsequently balance their tremendous experience with incredible ambiguity. That means, future justice, that you must endeavor to make sure that your past is free from anything that might define in no uncertain terms where you stand politically.

Having done that, you must then pander to a congressional committee that will ask you questions that you must strategically avoid answering at all costs. *What you say can and will be used against you.* Therefore, it is your duty—through a combination of Clintonian wordcraft and Reaganesque memory loss—to leave senators, journalists and the entirety of the American public scratching their heads with every answer.

If you've done your job right, your promoters will promote you and your detractors detract you based only on the tiny scraps of information that you have allowed to exist. Are you a hardcore conservative who aims to strike down *Roe v. Wade*? Are you a communist fifth column who wants to seize our guns? No idea. Matt Drudge might do his best to hint that you're a lesbian, but no one can do anything but guess where you will stand on abortion, gun control, eminent domain, campaign finance, freedom of speech, religion, immigration, governmental power or any other issues that may face the High Court.

That is, until you finally weigh in on your first case, which leaves one side screaming, "I told you so!" while the other just snickers . . . because no one can do anything about it.

HOME SWEET HOME

What Hollywood is to movies, the city of Washington, D.C., is to politics. It's the nation's administrative capital and also served for quite a long time as the nation's murder capital.

The city is not located in a state, but rather a federal district— hence the D.C. That designation means they have some weird features that separate them from other "normal" cities. One is that they have a single delegate to the House of Representatives, who can do pretty much what a member of Congress does . . . except, of course, vote. The other is that the city's mayor can be overruled by Congress. That's not a bad idea, seeing as Washingtonians once happily elected an ex-con who'd been videotaped smoking crack.

Unlike, say, the meandering city of Boston, with its wiggly, chaotic, cowpath roads, the city of Washington was thoughtfully planned. Since it was thoughtfully planned by a French guy, its design and architecture were clearly influenced by some of Europe's grand cities. It has wide avenues and low buildings that are reminiscent of Paris, which Thomas Jefferson was a big fan of long before it was *en vogue* to hate France.

It is here that you will find the home of the three branches of government—the executive branch's White House, the legislative branch's Capitol Building, and the judicial branch's Supreme Court of the United States. Being the nation's capital means it's chock full of beautiful monuments and some of the best art, science and history museums the country has to offer.

Drive around and you're sure to recognize a lot of famous names, but instead of George Clooney or Reese Witherspoon they're "Department of Energy" and "FEMA."

6

THE PARTIES
Celebrate the simplicity of lack of diversity

$\mathcal{Back}$ in the day when the country was still in its infancy and the British were licking their wounds, the concept of political parties was frowned upon, believe it or not. What the country's government needed, thought people like George Washington and Alexander Hamilton and Thomas Jefferson, was government by extraordinary individuals who were above the partisanship and chaos that political parties could bring. It was feared that parties might demand of a man (sorry, ladies!) that his allegiance be not to the United States itself but rather to an organization that might at times not act in the best interest of the country.

Seriously, the ability of these guys to predict things puts Jeane Dixon to shame.

Of course, human nature inevitably kicked in. As the country began to get its act together, people started having ideas of the way things should be. Some people, the Federalists, thought that a powerful central government was necessary to the growth of the country. Other people felt that a powerful central government would be too similar to the monarchy, which they'd recently given the finger.

Much like how new, uncertain parents bicker over whether watching *SpongeBob SquarePants* will ruin a child, the Founders and their fellow statesmen started to squabble over how the infant country should be raised. Faults began to form and one by one the great men (sorry ladies!) who ran the country began to polarize. Alexander Hamilton, who didn't like the idea of parties, became the leader of the Federalists. Thomas Jefferson was placed in the awkward position of hating the concept of political parties as he too formed a political party. Of course, any conflicted feelings he may have had about this double standard could presumably be easily overcome since he also happened to love liberty and keep slaves.

And so, in the late 1700s, human nature trumped all. The seeds for party politics were thus planted: the genesis of what would become the giant, money-sucking, disingenuous, self-pleasuring political monstrosities we've come to know and despise.

KEEPING IT SIMPLE

Many countries that have the terrible misfortune to not be America are plagued with a myriad of horrible things—not the least of which is that they're absolutely overrun with political parties. These parties range from those on the extreme right, who'd like you to go back to wherever you came from, to those on the extreme left, who pine for the proletariat. In between you'll find a mélange of right-leaning, left-leaning, centrist entities with pithy names like "Tory" or less pithy names like "Coalition of Truth and Experience for Tomorrow."

Some parties have large and diverse platforms that tackle numerous issues with varying degrees of vim and vigor, while others have circled their wagons around a single issue, such as marijuana, abortion, health care, secession, the environment, or, in the case of Denmark's "Party for the Animals"—animals.

It should be noted that when their organization is referred to as "single-issue," the spokeshumans at Party for the Animals wince and claim to possess other opinions as well. Though most people would probably agree that when you call yourself Party for the Animals you're setting yourself up as a single-issue party and are going to get what you deserve, no matter what your position is on torture, homelessness or the PATRIOT Act. Were I to start a political entity called Union of Coffee Haters, I would have no right to grimace when media labeled us a single-issue party, even if I also cared deeply about immigration reform and a flat tax.

Single-issue parties are as bad an idea as trying to paint a picture with only one color, or making iced tea using only ice. I'm going to go out on a limb here and assume you wouldn't marry someone just because of one single attribute that you happened to fancy, so why should you vote for someone who is laser-focused on a single issue? No good can come from it. Should the Green Party ever find itself in the position of helming the country (God forbid), it would soon find itself in countless uncomfortable scenarios. Faced with a showdown with some aggressor nation, one can imagine the newly elected Green president tearing his white-guy dreadlocks out at the realization that there's no such thing as an environmentally friendly battleship or a shade-grown, sustainable, fair-trade Predator drone attack.

WHY SINGLE-ISSUE PARTIES ARE A BAD IDEA

Dilemma	Pro-Life Party's Position
Russians invade Eastern Europe	They'd better not perform abortions.
Global warming melting ice caps	Hope flooding doesn't cause abortions.
Social Security goes bankrupt	Hopefully people won't seek abortions.
Iran goes nuclear	Let's make sure they don't get abortions.
Wall Street corruption fells economy	As long as there's no uptick in abortions.
Supreme Court rejects ban on abortion	Curses! What do we do now?

Despite the fact that single-issue parties aren't particularly useful, they continue to exist in countries all over the world, channeling their passions into a paragraph-size platform in the hopes that they can get voters so riled up about that one issue that they head to the voting booth to flip the switch, punch the chad, draw the X, touch the electronic-screen thingy or whatever it is people do in their voting booths these days.

Add all the single-issue parties to the numerous multi-issue parties and you have a big, gigantormous mess of parties of varying sizes, strengths and ludicrousness. Frankly, all these parties coming out of the woodwork tend to make politics very, very messy and terribly confusing. How can one expect to go about his or her life while at the same time keeping track of which party favors legalized prostitution and which party wants to gas feral cats?

Britain has something along the lines of 19 major political

parties. The wee nation of Israel, 12. Indonesia, 18. Chad, a country that no one really cares about and almost none of us could actually locate on a map, has 15. Just recently, 12 of Haiti's 18 candidates for president declared the election to be a fraud. *Eighteen candidates for president?* The only thing worse than having so many options to choose from is having only one to choose from, because that tends to mean you're living in a country where you're not likely to be voting anytime soon anyway. (*Looks over at North Korea.*)

When your country has an abundance of political parties, things get chaotic and confusing. Germany has a Christian Democratic Union and a Christian Social Union, which share some ideology with the Free Democratic Party, but definitely have a   ind with the Social Democratic Party. Trying to rememb for what is bound to get irksome and make anyor no wonder why in 1933 Germans simply threw up opted for the party with the funky logo whose lead

Alas, confusing, similar-sounding party name problem when you have a plethora of political pa You're going to have way too many billboards and bus ads and posters taped, stapled and glued all over the place. Imagine keeping track of all the political slogans, attack ads and pictures of smiling candidates! I've had the pleasure of being in several European countries during election seasons, and I can assure you that it's unnerving. Politicians leer at you from all angles, sporting subdued grimaces as they attempt to portray themselves as strong, noble, focused individuals with your best interests at heart. You simply can't keep track of them all, which explains why Europe keeps electing the people it keeps electing. The "feckless, vain and ineffective" (thanks, WikiLeaks!) Berlusconi comes to mind.

That is why America is better. In our very, very large country of more than 300 million very, very large people, we like to keep it simple. We've made it easy on our undereducated brains.

When it comes to major political parties, we have two.

THE TWO THAT MATTER

In America you are either a Republican or a Democrat. That's it. It really couldn't be simpler. There is one party to attend to all of your various viewpoints and represent you in government. It might seem impossible that one of those two parties could have a platform that you're wholly in agreement with, but it's true. And what happens if you're a Democrat who supports the traditionally Republican interpretation of the Second Amendment? Easy! You're a *moderate* Democrat. And if you're a Republican who believes in a woman's right to choose? You're a *moderate* Republican. Done.

America doesn't like people on the fence. If you claim to be anything other than a Democrat or Republican it's often viewed as a cop-out. An Independent is noncommittal in the same way that an agnostic is an atheist who is hedging his bets, or a bisexual is really just a gay guy in denial. When you tell someone that you're not a Republican or Democrat but rather that you identify with a third party or prefer independence, people will often raise one eyebrow like a Vulcan does and give you a look that's somewhere between "Wha—?" and "Are you absolutely serious?"

Let's face it. Having only two parties makes life easier for all of us. For one thing, it's easy to keep track of the party you hate—because it's the other one. It's far easier to direct all your anger and vitriol at one guy, rather than having to distribute it over a slew of parties like the Greens, the Reds, the Secular Christian Union Democrats, the Democratic Union of Secular Christians, Working Families and Workers' Rights. Too much choice results in options paralysis. Choice is a pain in the ass.

In America, this is how it works:

If you are Republican . . .

- You know that the Democratic Party is a bunch of amoral elitist ingrate snobs who sip overpriced chai soy lattes as they drive their hybrid cars from Karl Marx Fan Club meeting to vegan picnic to atheist study group.

- You know that between interracial orgies and Wiccan get-togethers, these liberal (read: socialist) America-haters are plotting ways to seize your bank accounts in order to pay for their pride parades, wind farms, abortions and reparations.

- You know these democrats (read: communists) are single-mindedly focused on seizing your guns, closing your church and demanding you assume financial responsibility for single moms and pay their union dues.

- You know they long for an inequality tax, a white-guy tax and mandatory participation in NPR Pledge Week (your $50 donation gets you a Ché shirt).

- You know progressive is code for sharia law, universal health care and open immigration.

- You have no doubts that democrats (read: Marxists) hate the military, God, baseball and would happily compost the original copy of the Constitution for their organic, sustainable hemp eco-garden. Also, talk radio would be banned, schoolchildren unionized.

- You know if you dare frown on their grand plans of these wily bastards, they'll hand your kids over to be raised by predatory gays.

If you are a Democrat . . .

- You know that the Republican Party is nothing more than a bunch of overweight, gun-toting Jesus freaks who shake their fists at the homeless.
- You know they suck on the teat of Fox News channel, lulling themselves to sleep at night by repeating the mantra "fair and balanced."
- You know they long for the days when people owned slaves and dinosaurs had saddles.
- You know they would like nothing more than to machine-gun seals, drill for oil in a national park and "turn Mecca into glass."
- You know that they'll hold up a misspelled sign.
- You know Republican women are hapless and subservient dupes who dream of homeschooling their twelve children so as to insulate them from the evils of public education, which is communism.
- You know that shouting "U.S.A.!" or waving a flag at a Republican will invoke a Pavlovian response.
- You know they'll gladly send their sons and daughters over to fight as long as you claim that Barbadians hate our freedoms—wherever Barbados might be.

See? Easy.

Sure, there are third parties in the United States, but when it comes to the American political system third parties are merely a little diversion—a snack before dinner—primarily because everyone knows third parties can't possibly win a serious election or ever do anything productive in the United States. It's no more logical than going to a Yankees–Red Sox playoff and rooting for the Orioles.

Because third parties defy our ingrained logic, they're often regarded as an entertaining freakish sideshow useful for breaking up the monotony of a typical election season. It's widely assumed that third-party candidates are just too insane to realize how absolutely perfect our two-party system is. As a government memo mentioned in 2009, people who follow third parties are likely to start militias and hide in a mountain cabin with their unvaccinated children, listening for black helicopters, hoarding muskets and printing their own currency.

The media love these delightfully hilarious candidates and invite them to debates and onto morning shows for a good chuckle. They let them speak their silly thoughts and make their silly cases and earnestly answer questions in debates; meanwhile the host stifles his laughter and resists the urge to turn to the camera and say, "Get a load of this guy!"

Billionaire Ross Perot entertained millions of us with the Kinko's pie charts he whipped up, offering up numerous folksy catchphrases like "giant sucking sound." But the sad truth, for Mr. Perot anyway, was that the whole time people watched and listened they were simply wondering at the end of the day how he would affect George H. W. Bush or Bill Clinton—because they were the only "real" candidates.

Indeed, when you mention you will be voting for a third-party candidate during any national election in this two-party country of ours, people will again raise one eyebrow like a Vulcan does and say something along the lines of, if not exactly, this:

"You're throwing your vote away."

Most Americans view voting for a candidate they believe in the same way they view professional soccer: *seems interesting, but no thank you.* Americans know full well that their mission as a voter is not about voting for a politician they adore but rather voting against a politician they hate. In fact, one of the more striking things about the 2008 election was that it appeared that the people voting for Barack Obama were doing so because they actually liked him as opposed to doing so merely to spite John McCain.

Let's be honest: Did the people who voted for John F. Kerry in 2004 really like him, as in Sally Field like-him-really-like-him? Or was it more plausible that they really, really couldn't bear the thought of George W. Bush winning a second term? Needless to say, people turned out in droves to vote against Bush, but Kerry—lacking any charisma gene whatsoever—didn't turn out enough anti-Bush voters. The end result was four more years of a president who could mangle a speech worse than the emcee at a cleft-palate convention.

Although third parties are the red-headed stepchildren in the United States, they do keep on trying, bless 'em. And every so often a third-party candidate shows up and runs a campaign effective enough that people are actually inclined to vote for him. The end result of this is always the same: One of the major party candidates loses and his supporters then blame the third party for drawing away valuable votes and "spoiling" the election. The most recent case of a third-party spoiler dates from the 2000 election, when the presidency was VP Al Gore's to lose.

Which he did.

Ralph Nader of the single-issue Green Party drew away exactly enough Democratic votes that the difference between Gore and

Bush the Second being president came down to who could out-maneuver whom in the courts. Despite lawyers being firmly in the pocket of the Democratic Party, the Republicans managed to squeeze out a victory and Al Gore embarked on a career terrorizing people with PowerPoint.

Let's get to know America's two major (i.e., only) political parties, as well as some of the ludicrous third parties that we all laugh and laugh and laugh at.

THE REPUBLICANS

The Republicans are represented by an elephant. An elephant, as we all know, is very large, gets poached for its tusks, has an excellent memory and freaks out when it sees a mouse. It's also followed by a guy with a large shovel and one of the worst jobs in show business.

Why Republicans chose an elephant to represent their party is anyone's guess, unless you actually can be bothered to go to Wikipedia to find out the answer, or what is believed to be the answer by the last fourteen-year-old to edit that particular entry.

The Republicans were the party of fiscal conservatism. I say *were* because lately they've had as much fiscal restraint as Donald Trump has had humility. Under George W. Bush in particular, the Republicans went batshit bonkers, spending money like there was no tomorrow because—spooked by the insane YouTube rants of nihilist Muslims—they presumably believed there might not actually be a tomorrow. George W. Bush, Republican, presided over one of the spendiest administrations ever, to the point where you could be forgiven for thinking that he was actually Ted Kennedy dressed as a swaggering Texan. Bush's legacy as King Spendy McSpenderson was brief, however, as Barack "I'll Have Two of Those" Obama immediately stepped in with the world's biggest credit card and began racking up reward points at your expense.

The Republicans fall on the right end of the political spectrum. Their stated interests are limited government, a strong defense, lower taxes and less dependence on government subsidy. They are largely associated with big business, entrepreneurs, the military, self-reliance, hard work, faith and patriotism.

Sadly, they're also associated with intolerance, insisting Darwin's theory was nothing more than a half-assed hunch, awaiting the triumphant return of the Lord and being terribly preachy about matters of the penis.

Some famous Republicans include the unsavory Richard Nixon and the much-beloved Ronald Reagan, who did or didn't fell communism, depending on which magazine you're reading. Many people forget that Abraham Lincoln was a Republican who devoted his presidency (and ultimately, life) to emancipating black people—so they could be free to vote solely for black Democrats like Marion Barry, Charlie Rangel, Ray Nagin and Kwame Kilpatrick.

I have a dream that someday the people who elect guys like this will transcend race and judge politicians not by the color of their skin but by the content of their character. It's probably worth noting that Martin Luther King, Jr. was registered as a Republican. Don't tell Barbra Streisand!

THE DEMOCRATS

The Democrats are represented by a donkey. Otherwise known as an ass.

You would think—you'd really think—that someone during the mascot brainstorming phase might have said something like "A donkey is an ass, I don't think we should have an ass as the mascot of our party." But no one did that. And donkeys are known for what exactly? Saying *hee haw* and pulling carts. It's a shame we couldn't all have been flies on the wall at that mascot concept session with some of the nation's most prestigious ad agency creative directors ruling out cats because they're pussies, lions because the English used them too much, bears because the Russians co-opted them, snakes because they're shady and eagles because they're too militaristic—but somehow ass made it through with flying colors. Apparently the Democrats vetted their mascot as well as the SEC vetted Bernie Madoff.

Democrats fall on the left end of the political spectrum. The party's stated interests are helping the less fortunate, equality and universal access to education and health care. They are largely associated with big cities, social justice, populism, the underdog and tenured professors.

Unfortunately, they're also associated with communists, political correctness, corrupt unions, emotion over logic, and taxing the living crap out of everyone.

AMERICA'S HILARIOUS AND ENTERTAINING THIRD PARTIES

Much like a ballistic missile shield, having a significant third party is something we give a lot of lip service to but deep in our heart of hearts acknowledge is just a lark. Nevertheless, we don't want to leave out America's political outcasts, because that would make them feel even more irrelevant than they already are, possibly causing them to mobilize and take up arms. Rather than risk the discomfort of a revolution, we give them hope and let them entertain themselves by rallying, getting excited every once in a while and blogging about it to their friends.

You may or may not have even been aware that some of these parties existed before, because depending on where you live in the United States, getting one on the ballot might be a Sisyphean task. The two-party system likes being a two-party system, and the one thing both Republicans and Democrats can really see eye to eye on is that it's in their best interest to keep competition to an absolute minimum. You can rest assured that whenever possible, your two major parties are working hard to make a three-party system a near impossibility. It's one thing they can be relied on to do very well.

THE LIBERTARIAN PARTY

The Libertarians like to call themselves America's largest third party and in fact might be, though it's really hard to say. Lots of people, like TV host Bill Maher, claim they're libertarian but in fact appear to be fair-weather libertarians who instead identify with only one or two popular libertarian ideals. In Maher's case, hookers and weed. Many people who call themselves libertarian wind up voting for Democratic or Republican candidates in major elections because they don't want to "throw away" their vote. So, they might be Libertarian-leaning but at the end of the day they're not Libertarian-voting, still siding with one of the country's two parties, which makes them "kind of" Libertarian at best.

Libertarians have the misfortune of having *liber* in their name, leading many people to assume they're "liberal" and therefore some kind of offshoot of the Democratic Party. They're not. A libertarian is best described as fiscally conservative and socially liberal. The Europeans call this political identity "classical liberal," though that's bound to confuse Americans even more than *Libertarian* already does. *Liberal* was made such a dirty word by America's right that even lots of liberals avoid using it, opting for *progressive* instead. That, or just admitting that they subscribe to *Mother Jones* and watch MSNBC.

As big fans of personal liberty, Libertarians are for limited government and against anything that infringes on one's right to do with themselves what they please—assuming it doesn't harm another individual. Libertarians are against drug laws, prostitution laws, gambling laws and seat belt laws.

They would just like you to leave them alone.

For this reason they attract no small number of druggies and anarchists, as well as conspiracy theorists and militia types. Naturally the media focuses on those highly entertaining fringe sideshows, which inevitably leads to a general tarnishing of the whole party as a bunch of absolute freaks.

The current darling of the Libertarian movement is Ron Paul, a Republican congressman from Texas who's earned the nickname "Dr. No" because he's a doctor, and he votes no on anything that doesn't meet his constitutional and Libertarian principles—which is almost everything. Including the war in Iraq. In the 2008 primary race Paul unnerved his Republican counterparts when he gained early momentum in the race. The media soon tired of covering what was dubbed the "Ron Paul revolution" and moved on. You may also have seen Ron Paul in the movie *Brüno*. After Sacha Baron Cohen's character came on to him, Paul freaked out and fled the interview.

THE GREEN PARTY

There's no reason to delve further into explaining the irrelevance of a one-issue party so we'll keep this short and sweet: Loving trees

and pandas and clean air is nice and you can score with girls who smell of patchouli, but it isn't really a good foundation for a political platform. If you're going to spend the bulk of your term in office turning off the lights in the West Wing and composting in the Rose Garden, you probably don't need to be anywhere near the Button.

That said, the Green Party's sometimes irrational concern for all things environmental is important since it does shed light on concerns and potential problems. This allows the two major parties to pay lip service to them and steal the good ideas, which they can then incorporate into their own platforms.

The most prominent Green Party member is 2000 presidential candidate Ralph Nader, who was vilified for helping Al Gore lose the election to George W. Bush. By voting for someone they actually believed in, the individuals who voted for Nader were not throwing their vote away, which is admirable, though they helped elect a lousy president, which is ironic and kind of unfortunate.

THE PROHIBITION PARTY

What can you say about a party founded on the idea that alcohol should be prohibited? Not only that, but one that pushes an idea that was tested between the years of 1920 and 1933 and failed miserably? And didn't just fail miserably, but caused crime to freaking skyrocket and leave behind a considerable body count?

Even though "the Noble Experiment" was finally repealed in 1933—to the delight of many millions—there is still, amazingly but I suppose not surprisingly, a Prohibition Party. Someone, somewhere, would like you to not be able to have a drink. That'd be for the health of society—and religious reasons, of course.

On their website, which looks like it hails from 1924, they claim to be the oldest third party in the country. Not sure if that's true, but any party without booze is certainly the lamest party in the country.

WORKERS WORLD PARTY

Like communists and film school professors the world over, the WWP lives in complete denial, insisting that communism has never really worked out the way communists think it should have. The theory's right, they say, it's just that the execution seems to have hiccups. There's something about handing a small group of people all the power that makes them not want to share it with anyone. Go figure. Despite the historical evidence to that fact, and the political philosophy's particularly heinous body count, they soldier on—whining about the exploitation of the proletariat and the coming worker's paradise and dreaming of a day when we can be as awesome as the Soviet Union was before it totally imploded.

DON'T GET TOO EXCITED

The preceding mention of some of America's third parties was solely for your amusement because if you're planning on participating in politics in America you'll need to decide which of America's two political parties best represents you. Until we're collectively able to get our act together, there are effectively only two parties.

PART THE THIRD

Washington, B.S.

Wherein we enter the bowels of the nation's capital
looking for "It" and investigate how "It"
permeates everything

7

THINK YOU'VE GOT ISSUES?
Baseball, hot dogs, apple pie and firearms

Every human who walks this earth comes with a mixed bag of issues. They hate the texture of mashed potatoes, agonize over touching restroom door handles, leap out of bed at the sound of dust falling, become maniacs when behind the wheel or derive erotic pleasure from sniffing shoes. Maintaining relationships with our friends and relatives often requires us to make concessions, to forgive and otherwise handle these issues as best we can, just as they surely go out of their way to accommodate, or forget about, ours.

Countries have their issues too. They range from the ones that irregularly appear and get under everyone's collar to the long-standing, festering ones that have the potential to split a country to the core: India and Pakistan have Kashmir. France has an abundance of nonassimilating North African immigrants. Greece and Turkey have the island of Cyprus. Australia has the Aborigines. Tanzania has some bizarre issue with Albinos. Russia, chronic vodka abuse. Saudi Arabia is petrified of women. North Korea is terribly insecure and lashes out when it needs attention.

Spin a globe, pick a country and if you're one of those folks who reads "all of 'em" newspapers, there's a very good chance you'll be able to call out one or two of that particular country's unique issues.

In America it's guns, gays, abortion, and the death penalty.

GUNS

From the perspective of our European cousins, when it comes to our issue with guns, America is clearly insane. That's an understandable position for them to take because they didn't grow up in a gun culture like we did. Sure, they had numerous bloody wars—including the biggest ones—fought on their various soils, but guns were never part of their culture in the way they were and are in ours.

During the early history of the United States, guns were a necessity, especially out on the frontier, where at various times one could expect to encounter hostile French, Spanish and British, as well as, of course, the natives whose territory we were encroaching on. Once the Europeans had been sent off (and the natives reduced in number and spirit), we had each other to worry about. As the old Time-Life commercial reminds us, one Wild West outlaw was "so mean he once shot a man for snoring." Who wouldn't want to be armed to the teeth in a world like that?

One thing is absolutely certain: No matter what your view is on the right to keep and bear arms, it just doesn't matter! Whatever your position is, some people will get very mad at you, other people will totally agree with you and absolutely nothing will come of it.

Though depending on your opinion, you'll either be labeled a "gun nut" or a "commie."

Anytime a lunatic shoots up a school or shopping center, the anti-gun crowd points fingers and shouts, "Look what happens when people have guns!"

Anytime a lunatic breaks into a house and shoots up a family, the pro-gun crowd points fingers and shouts, "Look what could have been avoided if they only had guns!" Expect it to continue like that for the next thousand years. You can thank the awkwardly written Second Amendment for creating just the right amount of confusion one needs to perpetuate this tug-of-war until the end of time.

Various states and localities with gun control in mind have tried making the process of purchasing a firearm so annoying that you give up, or have passed laws that later get struck down for their un-constitutionality. Depending on where you are in the United States at any particular moment, you might be able to carry a pistol with you into a Waffle House, or you might have to leave it in your glove compartment with the bullets in the trunk, or you might have to leave it at home. On the flip side of the restrictions, you have the city of Kennesaw, Georgia, famously passing a law in the early 1980s that actually *required* that homeowners possess a firearm.

You can argue that the Second Amendment was written back in the day when "arms" meant slow-loading, target-evading, misfiring muskets—and you'd be right. But you can also argue that it doesn't matter because the Constitution doesn't specifically rule out a fully automatic AK-47 assault rifle. So disagree we all will, though we can probably all agree that there's nothing more pathetic than a four-hundred-pound loner with a closet full of artificial manhood. Extra points if he has a Hummer in the driveway.

To say people feel very strongly about this issue is an understatement.

Lying in a hospital bed with gunshot wounds from a would-be assassin, and with his colleague James Brady paralyzed for life, Ronald Reagan still opposed gun control. Ten years later he would have a bit of a change of heart, encouraging Congress to pass the Brady Act, which required that gun purchasers wait five days to accommodate a background check.

As traditionally happens when it comes to any type of gun control efforts—no matter how reasonable they may seem to the non-pro-gun crowd—the National Rifle Association went into full offense. Its response was fast and furious and had lots of lawyers with big briefcases screaming about the Second and Tenth amendments.

"We just don't want bad guys and crazy people to buy guns," argued the supporters. Which is understandable. "We just don't want to wait five days to exercise our Second Amendment rights," argued the NRA. Which is also understandable.

And therein lies the problem.

The NRA eventually managed to get lawmakers to put in a sunset clause that would replace the five-day wait with an instant check done via computer. However, that concession still didn't stop them from suing up a storm, which ultimately led to a Supreme Court ruling that upheld most of the Brady Act, while agreeing with the NRA that *requiring* state and local officials to conduct background checks was unconstitutional. Said SCOTUS, the federal government could not demand that state and local officials comply. Unfortunately for the NRA, state and local officials didn't seem to mind complying. In 1998 the instant check went online and the five-day-wait argument was effectively lost. Faced with the prospect of arguing against relatively speedy sanity and criminal checks, the NRA backed off and their lawyers presumably bought very nice houses with all the money they made.

The Brady Handgun Violence Prevention Act has thwarted some two million illegal purchases, primarily by ex-convicts and fugitives from the law. Of course, despite that, bad guys still get guns, as we're reminded every time there's an incident with them. And there's nothing keeping a good guy with a gun from becoming a bad guy with one. As long as there are people with guns, people are going to argue the merits of people with guns. Good luck with that.

Guns are ingrained in the American psyche. Any mothers who have attempted to keep toy guns out of the house can only look on helplessly as their darling sons channel MacGyver and fashion weapons from tree limbs, Legos and cardboard paper towel tubes. If mom tries to enlist the husband for help, all he can offer is a shrug of the shoulders and the admission that he used to do the exact same thing.

As if to underscore the bizarreness of America's psychotic love/hate relationship with guns, the Brady Act's coauthor, Sarah Brady, caused a bit of a kerfuffle after it came to light that she'd *purchased a gun for her son as a gift*. That's right, the wife of James Brady—half of the nation's most prominent gun control advocating couple—bought her kid a gun. Even better, in doing so she avoided her son having to undergo a background check, effectively doing an end-run around her very own law. Not technically illegal, but it certainly makes you wonder.

GAYS

The gay-marriage debate introduces layer upon layer of delightful, mind-boggling complexity: Imagine, if you will, your laid-back, traditional Californian liberal, Obama-voting lifetime Democrat friend leaning over to tell you how absolutely against it he is. "I have no problem with gays," he tells you. "I have gay friends. I just don't believe in the marriage thing." And imagine his equally liberal wife next to him, nodding her head silently in agreement. True story. Happened to me.

Indeed, the opponents of gay marriage can't easily be pigeonholed because they're from all walks of life. So, in that sense they're of the same makeup as the supporters of gay marriage. They're Democrats, Republicans, religious, not religious, married, single. In the 2008 presidential campaign, candidates danced all over the place and when asked to clarify their position offered some variation on "I believe in tolerance . . . and that we should look into this later when the cameras aren't pointed at me."

In 2009, Miss USA contestant Carrie Prejean, lacking the verbal panache and prerequisite skills in lying that politicians have in abundance, was not so lucky. When semiliterate gossip hack, vulgarian and pageant judge Perez Hilton asked Prejean for her position on gay marriage, she answered honestly—stating that in her view it was between a man and a woman. Even though she followed up with "no offense to anybody out there," she was subsequently excoriated for her response. The resulting backlash ultimately led to her crown being taken back, albeit for an "unrelated" offense. Hilton, classy and eloquent as always, later called Prejean a "dumb bitch" and put her in the awful position of owing a favor to Donald Trump, who rode in on his toupee and valiantly came to her defense.

What's baffling about the Prejean drama is that her answer is the very same one that a majority of mainstream America offers up when they're asked. Including President Barack Obama. So who would pass Hilton's litmus test and not get called vile names?

Former first lady Laura Bush, sure. Oh, and Vice President Dick Cheney! He's been advocating for the federal government to get out of the marriage policing business since at least 2004. Only recently—February 2011—did the Obama administration take steps to do that by declaring the Defense of Marriage Act (1996—Clinton) unconstitutional and instructing the Department of Justice not to enforce it. It'd be cool if they did that with all the other unconstitutional laws on the books, but I digress.

What explains this bizarre mélange of gay marriage supporters and detractors? No idea! It's like people just consult their Magic 8 Ball. Should I support gay marriage? *Signs point to yes.* Should I oppose it? *Cannot predict now.*

While we can safely assume that most gays are in favor of gay marriage, that's where your reliance on the usual cast of supporters ends. Certainly blacks can relate to gays wanting to be treated equally under the law, right? No! Wrong! Ha! In California, 7 in 10 black voters supported 2008's Proposition 8, which defined marriage as being between a man and a woman. So while a majority of black voters identify with the Democratic Party and liberal politics in general, when it comes to gay marriage they draw the line. As one black voter told the *Los Angeles Times,* "I'm not really the type that I wanted to stop people's rights. But I still have my beliefs, and if I can vote my beliefs that's what I'm going to do."

Ironically, many blacks were at the polls that year specifically to vote for Barack Obama, so had there been a different candidate and the black turnout had been lower, Prop 8 might have failed. Or not: 53 percent of Latino voters supported the ban too. As did numerous religious groups such as Catholics, Mormons and Orthodox Jews. Even Hollywood's A-list celebrities running about, begging people to vote against the measure just wasn't enough. That's why this issue inevitably leaves you scratching your head, and any gay person looking around the room wondering what everyone is thinking.

Religious opposition to gay marriage is perhaps to be expected as religion and sex don't seem to mix well. But what about people who aren't particularly religious yet still oppose it? How do you explain your lefty Californian friend drawing a line in the sand? You'll hear a variety of reasons, from "gut feelings" to "sending the wrong message" to "going too far" to "slippery slopes." Former senator Rick Santorum caused a media frenzy after awkwardly opining that gay marriage could lead to people marrying dogs. Leave it to the pols to intellectually assess the situation. Woof!

One oft-cited reason is that marriage is for the purpose of procreation—something two men or two women are incapable of. Cop-out. Because if that's truly the case, heterosexual couples who aren't planning to have kids shouldn't be allowed to marry either. Ditto infertile ones, or those who are too old to have kids. Opponents will also point out that for thousands of years marriage has been between a man and a woman—and they have a point there. Proponents certainly did themselves no favor by demanding the instant sea change of such an established institution. But the notion that marriage is some pristine, holy alliance is somewhat diminished when you have bus ads touting ninety-nine-dollar divorces to remind us that half of all blessed unions end in failure. Every issue of *Us Weekly* or *In Touch* and every press conference featuring a philandering politician next to his unfortunate wife chips away at this sacred institution and leaves gay marriage opponents scrambling to bolster their argument. Or even better, trying to pull off the übercoup of amending the Constitution.

The concept of "civil unions" seems an appealing compromise to many—granting certain rights without calling it "marriage." That seems to ease the pain of making a decision on the issue for some. But there are plenty of others who insist that any kind of concession brings us one more step toward apocalypse. And plenty others say that this one small step would simply not be enough. Marriage confers more than 1,100 rights and privileges that civil unions do not, so if the civil union solution was a school paper, it would likely have "Needs Work" scrawled in red ink at the top.

Who's winning? Who knows. Unlike guns and abortion, with their clearly marked combatants, many of the factions in the gay marriage war refuse to wear uniforms and can blend in with the population. A victory on one side merely energizes the other and we find ourselves witnessing a debate that has more back and forth than a tennis match.

ABORTION

No other issue in American culture drives people as batshit crazy as abortion does. It's a third-rail issue in politics, the source of incredible amounts of vitriol and anger, and has spawned a cottage industry of maudlin bumper stickers, horrifically graphic posters and absolutely bizarre fetus dolls. To watch a campaigning politician tiptoe through this political minefield is one of the great joys in American politics, enabling us to learn from the masters themselves as they invoke their linguistic jujitsu to evade a straightforward answer to the simple question: *Are you for or against?* Only those politicians who are completely comfortable with their constituencies are willing to actually, truthfully define where they stand and opine whether *Roe v. Wade* was the greatest or worse thing to ever happen to America.

Best of all, it's an issue that cannot be resolved anytime soon because at its core it's a religious argument—and by virtue of being a religious argument relies on a wholehearted acceptance of something that has no physical manifestation. When does "life" begin?

Does a cluster of cells have a soul? What about an embryo three weeks after conception? Ten weeks? If there's no definitive answer to be had, no test results that will offer conclusive evidence, then it all comes down to faith: On one side, the belief that life begins at conception and abortion is then murder. On the other side, the belief that that's not true.

As with any argument where faith is a main factor, individuals have varying degrees of it and some can take it to the extreme, making it one political issue in this country that people are actually willing to commit murder for. That someone who is convinced that abortion is murder and that murder is bad would be willing to blow someone away would seem to be somewhat hypocritical. The murderer and his apologists will insist that this one murder prevented many other murders—much like choking baby Hitler to death would have. But in both cases, you have a lot of explaining to do.

To add to the confusion, of course, are the shades of gray. While the hard-core anti-abortion stance is *never under any circumstances,* there are more tempered varieties: *in cases of incest or rape* or *in the event of serious birth defects* or *if the mother's life would be in danger.* People and politicians frequently juggle these caveats depending on how their conversation is going.

The abortion argument has given birth to a wonderful game of semantics. There's *pro-choice,* which is handy if you want to emphasize that your opponents are against choice, or *pro-abortion* if you want to insinuate that an individual would run around discarding fetuses. *Anti-choice* makes the point that the other guys would tie your hands if they had their way, and there's *pro-life* to suggest that your opponents are pro-death. When things get ugly, the anti-abortion/pro-life folks break out the heavy guns and use *baby killer.*

The pro-choice/pro-abortion crowd has its own spectrum of

beliefs, from the "Abortion on Demand and Without Apology" crowd, which potentially views it as a form of contraception, to the individuals who find abortion distasteful but believe a woman's sovereignty over her body comes first. One thing is certain: A lot of individuals with strong opinions on abortion enjoy the luxury of never having to worry about one.

Especially the men.

Does removing the religious aspect that drives this argument make it any easier to handle? Not really. Our individual feelings and opinions about terminating a pregnancy are all over the map, influenced by numerous factors including but by no means limited to: family, social standing, intelligence, career, culture, tax bracket, philosophy, self-esteem, age—meaning you could be rabidly for or against abortion but find yourself completely and unabashedly changing your position the moment you're faced with the decision yourself.

In their 2005 bestseller *Freakonomics,* authors Steven D. Levitt and Stephen J. Dubner stated that a sharp decline in crime that began in 1992 correlated with the legalization of abortion eighteen years earlier. That probably wouldn't change anyone's stance on the matter, but it's definitely an interesting observation.

THE DEATH PENALTY

Capital punishment is a quandary factory, a grim enterprise that sets us apart from our European colleagues with whom we share so much and lumps us in with the less friendly, not-so-human-rights-oriented, not-so-convinced-life-is-valuable nations such as Iran, China, North Korea and Saudi Arabia.

Aspiring constitutional scholars can debate this issue to death (ha!). After all, if the Eighth Amendment prohibits cruel and unusual punishment, is killing someone not cruel? Is it not unusual? Hard to say, apparently, because the Supreme Court can't seem to agree. And this issue has bounced back and forth for a couple of centuries now. For the record, Founding Father lovers, Thomas Jefferson wasn't a big fan of it but his opposition efforts in Virginia were killed (ha, again!).

On one hand, dispatching a horrible villain would seem to appeal to our visceral desire for revenge, the pursuit of ultimate justice for the worst of our society. Did Oklahoma City bomber Timothy McVeigh not deserve to be terminated for his awful crime? Do two men who raped, strangled and torched a wife and her two young daughters belong on our planet? There's a case for letting people rot in prison for their entire lives. But it's also tempting to deny monsters their right to future sunsets. If they can see sunsets from their prison. Actually, if they can see sunsets from their prison I'd be pretty mad because they'd have a better view than I do.

But one can't help but feel some pangs of remorse, that sense that putting another human to death is a wee bit more sinister and less civilized than we'd like it to be. The long wait, the last day, the last meal, the last words and the desperate hope the governor will phone in with a last-minute reprieve—unless you're in Texas, in which case you know that's not happening. We try to make it better—devising more comfortable methods with which we can send the bad guys on their way, and indeed putting a criminal to sleep with a needle is far more "humane" than the shooting, stabbing and strangling that landed him in this predicament in the first place. But at the end of the day, it's the state-ordered killing of a human being, and you have to admit that feels a little weird. Not as weird as China's mobile execution vans, or Iran hanging people from construction cranes before morning prayers, but weird nonetheless. Like it or not, it's got some taint to it.

And there are the unknowns. What if the doomed man is the wrong guy? We know that prisoners on death row have been exonerated with new DNA evidence. The idea someone might be killed for something he didn't do is a horrible one and an uncorrectable injustice. What if the condemned finds himself there because of the malfeasance of a corrupt prosecutor? We know bad prosecutors happen all the time—remember the Duke Lacrosse scandal? What if the odds he's on death row were markedly increased because of the color of his skin? Uncomfortable questions.

The death penalty also makes for some awkward juxtaposition, such as the very common pro-life stance on abortion coupled with a pro-death penalty stance, which seems to suggest that all life is sacred but only sometimes. That has the same bizarre incongruity as a *Racist Civil Rights Activist* or *Pro-Meat Vegetarian*. Then again, this is all part of politics, and politics never seems to make much sense anyway.

THE OTHERS

America's a big country, so we are by no means limited in the number of issues that are known to torment us on a fairly regular basis. The severity of these arguments tends to wax and wane depending on several outside factors. During election years some issues come to the forefront because politicians, seeing that they can be employed against their opponents, pretend to be very interested in them. News events can also influence the import of various issues. Nobody gave two hoots about Islam until 9/11. The Department of Homeland Security (specifically the latex-fingered heroes of the Transportation

Security Administration) manages to outrage half the country every few months before being set aside. Same goes for the Federal Reserve, which we love when things are going well and absolutely hate when things aren't.

TAX REFORM

It's widely understood that Republicans pretty much hate anything to do with taxes and that Democrats—ever the paragon of tolerance—are much more receptive to them. It's safe to say that most Americans agree that taxes are necessary. They like having police departments, highways and nice battleships. It's harder to get them to agree on who should be paying those taxes, or how much tax they should be paying. Or what type of tax it should be. Tax reform is a popular election-year issue as talk of "fixing a broken system" tends to rally the troops. There'll be talk of flat tax, European-style Value Added Tax (VAT) and cutting or changing this, that or the other tax. At around eighty thousand pages, the U.S. Internal Revenue Code is appalling and the bureaucracy that enforces it is one of this country's bigger boogeymen. In fact, if you were to offer Americans the choice between eliminating the IRS or Al Qaeda, I'm betting there would be a lot of discussion and weighing of risks versus benefits.

Whatever a politician's opinion of taxes may be, there has been a strong bipartisan effort to avoid personally having to pay them. From members of Congress who write our tax laws, to the people in the administration who enforce them, there's no shortage of individuals regretting their "unintentional" and "careless" errors. Treasury secretary Timothy Geithner was lucky in that his tax woes didn't prevent him from being sworn in. And he was even luckier that the IRS didn't assess him any penalties—as they would have for any average American citizen. Like you. Or me. This particular act of leniency prompted some enjoyable political theater when two Republican congressmen announced that they would be introducing the Geithner Penalty Waiver Act.

IMMIGRATION

Anyone who has firsthand experience with America's immigration system can tell you that it is terribly, terribly, terribly broken. I have firsthand experience, and I concur. Any system that punishes you for playing by the rules and rewards you for breaking them? Broken. Let us not forget that six months after Mohamed Atta and Marwan Al-Shehhi flew planes into the World Trade Center, they were issued visas. Happened to be at the very same time my wife and I were dealing with the dreadful INS—predecessor of the USCIS.

We are the most diverse country on earth. My building's doormen: Guyana, Poland, Puerto Rico, Florida. My tailor: China. My dry cleaner: Honduras. Neighbors: Bangladesh and India. Corner store: Syria. Not to mindlessly cheer "Celebrate Diversity!" because diversity certainly has problems not worth celebrating, but I do feel that my children benefit strongly from their exposure to the people, habits, foods and cultures of the world.

There is perhaps some hypocrisy in a nation born of immigrants complaining about immigration, but the issue comes back time and again. In the 1800s it was the Irish and Germans who got under everyone's skin. Now the descendants of those unwanted Irish and Germans are firmly ensconced in all aspects of American society from entertainment to business to sports and certainly politics— Kennedy, anyone?

Today's unwanted immigrants come from all over the globe.

Some are more unwanted than others, it seems, and plans for doing something about it vary. Many immigrants suffer the plight of being wanted *and* unwanted. As in we really need them to do certain jobs, but we're just not crazy about them being here to do them. This would seem to send mixed messages.

Whenever the topic of illegal immigration comes up, most people tend to think of Mexicans. That makes sense: We share a border with their country, there is what you might call an "incentive" to get the hell out of that country, there are lots of them here already and the penalty for coming here illegally has generally been the equivalent of MSNBC hosts Keith Olbermann and Joe Scarborough's micro-suspensions: "Don't do that again please, thank you, bye."

We don't seem to be as concerned with Canadians streaming across the border. And they seem to be happy there, so they don't. Ironically, the folks coming up illegally from Mexico are generally doing so to make a better life. One of the more famous illegal immigrants coming down from Canada, jihadist Ahmed Ressam, was doing so to take lives.

What does seem to be different these days is that the immigrants of yesteryear were keen to assimilate into society. They pushed their children to adopt the English language, to embrace and fit in to American culture. And they did. These days one gets a sense that adopting the culture is not as important or is even disdained. This manifests itself in parents pushing for schools to teach their own native tongues, or adopt their own mores and defer to their values. It's a pattern seen in Europe, and as we've seen in Europe, that pattern isn't particularly pretty.

During elections in New York City, signs directing voters to polls say "Vote Here" in English, Spanish, Korean and Chinese. That might be a little too accommodating. If you don't even know what "vote here" means in English, how can you be expected to know much about the candidates, the issues or the ballot initiatives?

Fixing immigration won't be easy, particularly because ultimately Americans want cheap strawberries and landscaping. Coming down hard on the issue will please some groups, as happened in Arizona, but will also alienate the growing Hispanic base—something most politicians will be increasingly loath to do as that base grows. Suggest that illegal immigrants should be given driver's licenses, like disgraced former New York governor Eliot Spitzer did, and you'll touch off a firestorm. And not doing anything at all presents risks to the culture, the economy, and national security. No easy fix to be found, but rest assured we'll get lip service about it whenever it's required.

MEDICARE REFORM

Reforming an entitlement like Medicare is like being one hundred years old and in full possession of your mental capacities. You realize that you could be dead at any moment—but you'd rather not think about it. So you go about your business and hope that today's not the day. However, no matter what you're up to—whether you're making a sandwich, watering a geranium or getting ready for bed—there's a little voice in the back of your head going, *it could be any moment now.*

And so it is with Medicare. The optimists among us aren't worried and are convinced they'll live to see another day. The pessimists are worried they'll drop dead any moment. Nobody wants to think about it.

And rightly so. The mere mention that you might be fudging with someone's golden-years perks is death for politicians. Oh sure, they might agree with you that *something* needs to be done, but reach toward any of *their* precious benefits and you'll have AARP members gnawing through your arm. Don't forget, people like getting "free" things; they just don't like when other people get them.

Unlike Social Security, which is or isn't in peril depending on your party affiliation, both Republicans and Democrats seem capable of acknowledging that as more and more people continue to live even longer lives, Medicare's going to get even more outrageously expensive. This leaves politicians with an unfortunate quandary: Raise taxes and suffer the slings and arrows of outraged citizens or cut benefits and suffer the slings and arrows of outraged citizens. Really, the best and most manageable option would be cleaning the slate with a lethal supervirus that wipes out everyone over forty. But don't get your hopes up.

EDUCATION

The battle over public education has been heating up as of late. This is partly due to the Internet exposing us to incredibly large numbers of dumb people with dumb ideas, dumb comments and an inability to express them properly.

The Republicans have been pissing and moaning about the Department of Education ever since Jimmy Carter signed it into existence, while the Democrats have in general been big fans, as public education incorporates several things that Democrats are often caught having erotic thoughts about: multiculturalism, universal accessibility and unions.

However, after three decades of screaming "Throw more money at it!" and achieving no perceivable results, most individuals have arrived at the conclusion that money is not necessarily the answer and that the educational system is in need of overhaul. One of the biggest obstacles has been the teachers' unions, who've fought any significant change tooth and nail. After decades of taking intractable positions such as protecting truly awful teachers from being fired, valuing seniority over ability and refusing any kind of "merit" pay system, they finally seem to have crossed some imaginary line and outraged just enough people. Director Davis Guggenheim's 2010 film *Waiting for 'Superman'* was a call to arms that took the broken system to task and made no bones about faulting the teachers' unions for their betrayal of our children. What makes the film particularly interesting is that its very existence indicates a rift between the left and the teachers' unions. That's because Guggenheim has some serious left-wing credentials as director of *An Inconvenient Truth* and a short film about Barack Obama. That résumé didn't faze conservative commentators one iota: *Waiting for 'Superman'* received rave reviews by some of the same folks who had openly mocked Guggenheim and Al Gore just four years earlier. What makes this exciting to the outside observer is that it would seem to suggest the possibility of a noble bipartisan effort to reform America's unhealthy educational system. A very welcome development that might help us fend off the epidemic of stupid we're experiencing, as evidenced by the existence of an iPod app called Fruit Ninja and the film *Jackass 3D*.

Change we can believe in, let's hope.

OF COURSE THERE'S MORE

Are you kidding me? We could go on for weeks! Cap and trade. Line-item veto. Torture. School prayer. Farm subsidies. Living wage. Pledge of Allegiance. Food stamps. Ten Commandments. Assisted suicide. Amnesty. Ethanol. Tort reform. Drilling. Estate tax. Global warming. Deficit reduction. Gerrymandering. School vouchers. Border fences. Solar power. Stem cells. United Nations.

So much to complain about.

Options paralysis? Don't you mind. Pick the ones that get you the most excited and surely someone else will find joy in others. As the saying goes, "One man's eminent domain is another man's single-payer health care."

8

MAKING THE RULES
Law and odor

When Charlton Heston came down from the mountain with the Ten Commandments he was introducing the rule of law to the Israelites, which perhaps explains why so many of them went on to become lawyers. The one about not killing people is a pretty nice law, one has to admit. It was that sentiment that went on to inspire a variety of laws that today are the only reasons why Kanye West and Rosie O'Donnell haven't been strangled by mobs.

Most of us are grateful to live in a society that has some semblance of law to it, and citizens who respect the really important ones for the most part. Compared with other parts of the world, we're doing quite nicely, and you can pretty much count on being able to leave the house without being shot, stabbed, beheaded or set on fire. We have some nice laws that work very hard to keep everyone civilized, and that's always a good thing. The alternative, anarchy, is unpleasant. The only anarchist I ever met was in college and I'm pretty sure he didn't understand what anarchy actually was—he just liked drawing the Ⓐ symbol on the walls, which ironically was against the rules. Most sensible Americans (or sensible anybodies, for that matter) would find real anarchy, the Waziristan tribal region kind of anarchy, pretty depressing. Nothing good ever comes from lawlessness and warlords.

We're glad to have some kind of recourse if someone like Bernie Madoff steals our life savings, or if actor Vincent Gallo sets our house on fire or rapes our cat. For a society to be prosperous requires some semblance of a legal structure. The security of knowing that your property can't be stolen from under you, that your business can't be seized, that corruption is tamed. It's why international conglomerates base their operations in New York City and not Mogadishu. Or Chicago. No, I kid: Chicago may have legendary, entrenched corruption, but at least there are actual laws being broken. Mogadishu doesn't even have laws. Or functioning traffic lights.

KNOW WHEN TO SAY WHEN

Of course, at some point there is such a thing as too much law. Dictating the curvature of a banana for sale, for example. Requiring a label in eight languages to let people know hot coffee is hot. Anyone who's tried to open a business can tell you that there are probably too many local council laws dictating everything from sign size to paint color to the type used on the menu. I know several entrepreneurs and there's never a shortage of complaints about pencil-pushing bureaucrats holding things up for a variety of reasons, many of which come down to too many half-assed laws, arbitrary enforcement of said laws or a dysfunctional bureaucracy that can't be overcome because the law is on their side. I was profoundly excited to learn that an Irish pub was opening in my neighborhood. I remember the COMING SOON sign, and the construction. I remember looking in the window at a gorgeous bar. And I remember walking by regularly and wondering when the hell that bar was going to open. It didn't make any sense! They were clearly ready to open, yet for month after month it sat there, ready and empty. When I finally chanced to encounter someone acquainted with the place and asked what was going on, I got the answer I had started to suspect: "It's the city," they sighed. Rather than let the bar open the city dragged its feet. Rather than let a business finally open up that was ready to give people jobs and contribute valuable tax dollars to the city's coffers, the bureaucracy and its underlings plodded along, created obstacles, changed demands, gave conflicting answers and caused a lot of headaches. Not to mention the ulcer-inducing stress of paying months and months of exorbitant New York City rent on a place that was generating zero income.

But all of these annoying local laws that plague us in hamlets, villages, cities and towns across the country absolutely pale in comparison to the whoppers capable of being envisioned, promoted and passed by the United States government. Time and again, in an effort to make the country a better place and, more important, to justify their positions as lawmakers, they come up with some of the most incredible ideas ever conceived in the history of thinking stuff up. They tell us how great it will be when the idea becomes a law, and then they turn the idea into a law with great fanfare, often without having the slightest concept of what the new law might actually wind up doing. And we all know how that tends to end.

INSPIRATION

Where do our nation's laws come from? Our lawmakers, of course! On the federal level that means the noble men and women of the United States Congress. And of course, our modern presidents are certainly ready, willing and able to come up with their own brilliant ideas, and often do.

Politicians are like musicians or poets—these talented souls can find creative inspiration in even the most mundane things. But unlike musicians or poets, politicians can turn their inspiration not into a song or poem, but into a federal law! And unlike a song we don't have to listen to or a poem we don't have to read, a real federal law is something we're going to have to deal with day in and day out until it's repealed, like it or not.

The people who make the laws that the rest of us must contend with are inspired by a desire to make their mark on history, correct a real or perceived injustice or protect us from a real or imagined danger. Their intentions may be noble, not so noble, kind of noble, or there are no intentions. In those instances the laws are simply cerebrally unsound knee-jerk reactions to something that with the benefit of time and afterthought doesn't make much sense. Kind of like the way airport security personnel wanted to deprive my infant son of the bottle he was drinking from in the aftermath of the failed 2006 airline "peroxide" bombings.

At the rare times when inspiration is waning, politicians need not fret. Writers may suffer writer's block, and presumably musicians and poets suffer song block and poem block, respectively. But there's no such thing as law block! If a politician isn't feeling creative he or she can always count on a vast army of lobbyists to offer up a clever idea or two as well.

"Why not require that gasoline be made with corn?" whispers the lobbyist.

"Great idea!" says the excited, well-meaning politician.

And so a new law is born. Before you know it a food source is being diverted into an energy source that many scientists think has zero, or even negative, benefit. Oh, and the supply of corn goes down and the price of corn goes up.

BONUS

Getting a law passed often ensures you'll be remembered long after you've left the hallowed halls of Congress. It's been more than nine years since Representative Michael Oxley cosponsored a bill with Senator Paul Sarbanes. The duo both left politics in 2007 but they're still fondly remembered by businesses throughout the country as the men responsible for Sarbanes-Oxley, a law that sought to eliminate corporate fraud by creating incredible amounts of crippling paperwork and ultimately encouraging some companies to take their business to the London Stock Exchange instead. But that's a small price to pay for the knowledge that they may or may not have curbed some corporate fraud. Has it curbed enough fraud to justify the time and expense required to abide by the law? Hard to say, because if it actually prevented fraud, we don't have anything to point to. That allows its supporters to say yes, and its detractors to say no! *Hooray!*

WHAT'S IN A NAME?

It might seem counterintuitive but a career in politics is the perfect choice for the remarkably creative individual. Politics offers endless opportunities to flex your creative muscles, whether you're trying to evade answering a question, explain why you inexcusably pardoned a complete scoundrel, justify a war or need to convince skeptics you're a God-fearing churchgoer.

But the creative spirit isn't only on display at press conferences or while you're getting grilled by Morley Safer on *60 Minutes*. It's also prevalent behind closed doors. In subcommittees, for example, where, seated around a presumably expensive table, you're tasked with coming up with a clever name for your bill.

It is here that ingenuity truly bubbles to the surface and enters the world of wordcraft—the linguistic camouflage aimed at masking a bill's true identity. Any potential opponent is blissfully unaware of what is in his midst.

This wordsmanship employs the same kind of truth stretching favored by real estate professionals, in whose reality "adjacent to a waste treatment facility" is "waterfront" and a hole in the roof is "airy." In addition to using words that would seem to be unrelated to the legislation's intention, politicians get extra points if those misleading and inaccurate words form a clever acronym.

For a great, fairly recent example of this creative artistry let's imagine a hastily assembled piece of legislation that in a frantic effort to "keep us safe" effectively drops its trousers and takes a big ol' poop on the Constitution and our civil liberties. You wouldn't call it the Poop on the Fourth Amendment and Hold People Indefinitely Act because that's too honest, and the acronym POFAHPI sucks. What's a good name-comer-upper-with supposed to do? You have to ask yourself some questions:

What does this legislation do? Well, it dramatically reduces the restrictions placed on authorities for obtaining intelligence from individuals, infringes on your privacy in myriad ways, allows suspects to be held indefinitely and generally encourages traipsing all over the Fourth Amendment. Therefore, it's clearly UNITING AND STRENGTHENING AMERICA.

And why do we need to unite and strengthen America? To keep us safe, of course! And we keep ourselves safe by giving the government carte blanche to do what it needs to unite and strengthen America. If that means holding someone indefinitely based on secret evidence they won't show you, preventing you from opening a bank account using a PO box as an address or letting Uncle Sam look at the library books you've been checking out—well then, we're just PROVIDING APPROPRIATE TOOLS.

And these tools that expose citizens and foreigners alike to all this unpleasant intrusion, that laugh at our Constitution and that have all these civil rights people screaming and hollering bloody murder as a result—what are they going to do? Oh, glad you asked. These tools will INTERCEPT AND OBSTRUCT TERRORISM!

And now it starts to become clear. It may be a tremendous, ridiculous mouthful but there you have the largely unread and hastily rubber-stamped Uniting and Strengthening America by Providing Appropriate Tools Required to Intercept and Obstruct Terrorism Act. USA PATRIOT! How could you disagree with an acronym like "PATRIOT"? That would be as un-American as . . . well, let's not go there.

THE HITS KEEP COMING

The USA PATRIOT Act is merely one great, bipartisan chart-topper in a string of boldly and brilliantly named hits. If only it were a hard act to follow. Alas, the juggernaut is unstoppable, the hitmakers putting their skills to the test and delivering us one masterpiece after another. Like the Beatles, but with less emphasis on harmony.

Under the National Labor Relations Act there's a standard procedure to organize a union. The organizer acquires signatures of the majority of employees saying that they want to unionize. He delivers the signatures to the management. Management holds a secret ballot—to make sure that no one was bullied or pressured into signing the cards. If the ballot reflects that a majority of employees still want to be unionized they go to the bargaining table.

Now imagine a bill that would eliminate that secret ballot. If a union organizer rounds up enough signatures, off to the bargaining table they go. Doesn't that mean that employees could be pressured/annoyed/threatened into signing the cards? Sure. What do you call this piece of legislation then? The EMPLOYEE FREE CHOICE ACT.

You're scratching your head, right? Don't stop! The largely divisive, recently enacted health-care reform legislation lacks a clever acronym with PPACA, but the Patient Protection and Affordable Care Act makes up for it with a name that suggests it protects patients and is affordable. It protects some patients, sure, just not the ones who aren't going to be covered because their insurance is dropping them. Or the million-plus patients whose employers received waivers. Or the estimated 23 million who won't be covered when the law takes full effect. And as far as "affordable" goes—the country still has to pay for it somehow. Calling it affordable displays a level of optimism that hasn't been seen since Neville Chamberlain flew back to England from a meeting with Hitler in 1938 and told everyone not to worry.

THE LAW OF UNINTENDED CONSEQUENCES

Creating laws requires a foresight that our Founding Fathers seem to have had in abundance but that our current lawmakers sorely lack. As they pursue their utopia they never seem to take into account human nature, or the nature of business. As many of our politicians have never actually owned anything remotely like a business, this is pretty understandable.

The planet that many lawmakers live on is different than the one you and I inhabit. It looks like ours and seems like ours in many ways, but on their world there are no variables, no surprises. Everything happens exactly as one had imagined it was going to happen. The people go about doing what one thinks they're going to do; they respond exactly as one imagined they would. There are no contingencies to prepare for. For every action there is no opposite reaction. The laws of physics are different there, even though Einstein said they should be the same everywhere in the universe.

To better understand the world Congress lives in, and the trouble they keep getting us into, imagine your friend is driving you from point A to point B in a terrible snowstorm on a desolate highway. Along the way, the tire goes flat.

"Should we change the tire?" you ask.

"I don't have a spare," your friend informs you.

"Why don't you have a spare?" you demand.

"Didn't think I'd need one," is the answer.

"Call Triple-A!" you bellow.

"I left my phone at home in case I couldn't get a signal out here."

"Do you have flares?"

"No, because I thought we'd only be on the road for an hour."

"Then go get help!"

"No jacket," your friend informs you. "I really wasn't expecting to have to go outside. And I'm wearing sandals."

The world we inhabit is different. A little grittier. More real. We don't share the same sense of boundless optimism that our current Floundering Fathers have. We know that people never behave the way we expect them to. We believe in luck, good and/or bad. We expect things to go wrong not because we're inherently cynical but because they've gone wrong in the past and we remember the occasion. Past experience tells us that politicians seldom learn from past experience and have absolutely no knack for prediction. Far too many of them are fully capable of dousing themselves with gasoline, leaping over a campfire and being genuinely surprised at the result.

And yet these are the people coming up with the ideas for the laws, passing the laws and watching, often with long faces, as the laws don't do what they were supposed to. And after the initial realization and disappointment come the recriminations and the excuses. The Democrats didn't believe in Tinker Bell enough, so she disappeared . . . The Republicans had no intention of helping the Ewoks . . . And after the finger-pointing and spin comes the fix— inevitably a new law. Wash, rinse, repeat.

Prohibition is one of the grand examples, but there's no shortage of laws not doing what they're supposed to have done. Mandatory minimum sentencing and three-strikes laws have put people in jail for life, even in cases where life sentences are absurdly disproportional to the crime. Consumer laws have destroyed businesses. Punitive antismoking laws have created black markets. You name it, there's a law for it, and the law's doing something that the creator of the law didn't foresee.

FUN WITH NUMBERS

When politicians have a law they would like to pass they first need to convince Americans and a majority of their colleagues in Congress that passing that law is a great idea. They do this by telling them all the wonderful things that the new law will do for the country and her citizens; making our lives better or safer is a popular approach.

One of the most important things politicians must bear in mind, though, is that cost is very important to Americans, therefore their new laws should not be expensive. Fortunately they never are! This is perhaps the only time in his career that a politician is genuinely optimistic.

The price tag of a new law is arrived at through a combination of unbridled optimism, untruthfulness, fuzzy math, wholly defective logic and a total departure from reality. Armed with this acceptable number, the politician can then address the American people and reassure them that this law will not break the bank. Having thus persuaded us, he sees his bill become law. Not long afterward—usually minutes—everyone comes to the grim realization that it's going to be twenty times more expensive and that it seems they've been had. Much like a spouse caught in the cycle of domestic abuse, we seem surprised that this is happening once more. *You said you would change!* we think to ourselves, as our self-esteem suffers another blow for having let ourselves get suckered yet again.

NOT THE OTHER WHITE MEAT

In 2010 there were 9,129 projects known as "earmarks"—the nice way of saying "pork"—which refers to the egregious placement of little paragraphs inside huge pieces of legislation that result in, say, a bridge being built in the desert. Everyone agrees it's bad, so naturally no one can seem to decide what to do about it. In the 2010 midterm elections, one of the Tea Party's causes was such earmarks.

Of course its appealing—taking $7 million in taxpayer money to pay for a grant or building with your name on it.

Pork turns even the most staunch fiscally conservative Republicans into raging welfare queens. The government's giving away money? Gimme some of that. What better way to please your constituency than to bring millions of dollars of construction projects into your state.

LOBBYISTS

Lobbyists are like the people who pen hit songs for people like Britney Spears and Justin Bieber. You don't always see them, but you're familiar with their work. They're nothing new either. During the Constitutional Convention the doors were bolted and the windows shut (in the middle of the summer, remember) in an effort to prevent outside influence from mucking up the proceedings. That's probably why the Constitution wound up being short and sweet and entirely lacking in special provisions for sheep farmers, blacksmiths, Protestants and people of Dutch descent.

Today, lobbyists have multiplied like rabbits. They outnumber members of Congress at an alarming rate, swarming all over D.C. in business suits and skirts, armed with large briefcases and BlackBerrys and lists of politicians they need to corner. They represent trade groups, special interest groups and social policy groups of all sorts and all sizes. You name it, and there's probably someone on K Street in Washington, D.C., who has a cozy office devoted to shopping it around the nation's capital. They meet with lawmakers and ply them with research and policy papers that defend their position. Whether seeking subsidies for pineapple farmers, higher immigration quotas for people from Madagascar or casinos at every highway rest stop, they argue their cases and try in earnest to get the politician to see things their way. They wine and dine and schmooze and donate and fund-raise for candidates and generally do whatever it takes to avoid what they do being seen as bribery.

Some lobbyists are tremendously powerful, holding their enormous memberships over the heads of nervous, trembling politicians. Many of these groups issue "report cards" to members, summing up a politician's voting record on their issue; no matter how much a lawmaker may have agonized over his yea or nay vote, it's ultimately reduced to the simplicity of an A or D grade. The simplicity of a letter grade is much better for the instant formation of strong opinions like *He's a gun nut* or *He hates old people.*

Speaking of: the American Association of Retired Persons can, with a single press release, raise an army of 35 million undead to torment and terrify entire blocs of Congress. If you think your dad could bitch up a storm, just multiply him by 35 million and imagine the thunderous, bowel-shattering auditory assault they're fully capable of. And those folks are retired, so they certainly have plenty of time to complain until you finally cave in.

Groups like AIPAC, the American Israel Public Affairs Committee, have incredible leverage. Deep pockets give them the ability to reward legislators who are on board and punish the ones who aren't by funding their political opponents. With that kind of clout, it's no wonder AIPAC has had what's been described as a "stranglehold" on Congress. If you've ever wondered why American policy toward

Israel often seems self-defeating and nonsensical, well, you simply just don't recognize really good lobbying in action.

PERMANENTLY TEMPORARY

In an effort to tamp down any resistance and pass unpopular legislation, our nation's lawmakers will often endeavor to soothe us with the assurance that the unpopular law is only necessary for the time being. As soon as it's done doing what it's supposed to do, we are told, the law will be repealed. If we really need convincing, they'll even offer us a "sunset clause" for when the law will actually repeal itself.

If a deranged person with torn clothes and a bloody knife leaps into our car and tells us to drive deep into the woods, we probably have an idea of what's coming. He can tell us "I'm not going to hurt you" over and over again, in as calm a voice as one can muster when holding a bloody knife, but we're not buying it. For some reason that same, rational gut instinct fails us almost every time when dealing with politicians.

"It's just for the time being," they tell us, raising one eyebrow a little suspiciously. But not suspiciously enough, I suppose, because we nod our little heads and hold up our little thumbs and give them the green light. Then, years later, when the law is still on the books and annoying the hell out of all of us, we remember that the law was supposed to have had a short life, like a May fly, and we try to get the attention of the politician who so dearly needed it last time, so that we might just remind him of that fact. But, like a waiter who is too busy and can't be bothered to trifle with the likes of you, he simply pretends not to see you gesturing and waving your empty glass and instead bolts into the kitchen.

The number of temporary tax laws still on the books is staggering.

Brought on by some economic malaise (i.e., the inability to honor a budget), they are introduced to us as "emergency" measures designed solely to get us through hardship. Failure to do so, we are told, could bring disaster upon us. Firefighters will be laid off and trash will rot on the side of the road. Wild gangs will roam the unplowed streets and the police, unable to afford bullets or handcuffs, will only be able to stand idly by as you are beaten to death in front of your family. Bridges will collapse, sinkholes will form, water will stop running and civilization as we know it might very well come to an end.

To your credit, you protest a bit—you've been bitten before—but the politician counters. With the sincerity of a gambling addict determined to change his ways if only you'll bail him out of his troubles this time, he pleads. It won't happen again. It's only a *teeny weenie* little tax. A small price to pay to get us out of this rut. And it's *temporary* until we can "get spending under control." You acquiesce. The tragedy is averted.

But, they soon learn, the extra cash in the coffers is kind of nice to have. It can buy things. Soon it's appropriated for other uses and the idea of eliminating the tax right now is unfeasible, for that might lead to a deficit. As time progresses and since the politician who proposed it has left politics altogether, the tax becomes a foundation to be built upon. It's certainly not enough as is, so the rate is raised a bit (albeit with the promise of the hike being only temporary, if you object loudly enough). Half a century later the tax is still there and any suggestion that it be struck down is scoffed at because money's in short supply. You can't complain anymore—you're dead—and your children have lived with it their whole lives anyway. For them, just as with the Internet and not having to pay for a newspaper, it's something that's always been there.

The Current Tax Payment Act of 1943, which reinstituted a with-holding tax under the justification of wartime expenses, is one of the most oft-cited examples of temporary laws that aren't temporary, but the Eternal Law is not limited to taxation. The aforementioned, lovely PATRIOT Act had a sunset clause. The sunset clause existed to calm the nerves of those of us worried that such hastily prepared, sweeping, undeliberated legislation tossed together in the panicky days following the national trauma of 9/11 might be dangerous. It's *temporary*, we were told. In four years it will begin to dissipate into the ether. Your fears are unfounded. Rights you hold sacred will be restored. Okay, we said, still jittery about this most horrific attack on our country.

Four years later, their heads clear and nerves calm, the legislators set out to undo the sunset clause and make the legislation perma-nent—and we were left with the realization we'd been had, yet again.

9

How a Bad Idea Becomes a Regrettable Law

From genesis to ugly revelation

𝕶nowing what we know from the previous chapter, let us take a hypothetical look at the birth and life of dreadful legislation. This exercise should leave us with some insight into how the game in Washington is played, and how a bad idea someone had goes on to become a terrible, terrible law that everyone absolutely hates. Please remember: This is a hypothetical creation, not a real piece of legislation. You are well advised to avoid citing it in any school papers.

Ben Bumblebrook is a congressman from the great state of wherever. He's eager to take advantage of his newly acquired public office to serve his public (he's a public servant, remember). He would love to improve the lives of his constituents and make the country better, stronger. It also wouldn't hurt to make a name for himself in the process.

One fine afternoon during the workweek (Tuesday through Thursday on Capitol Hill), Congressman Bumblebrook finds himself once again engaging in extramarital sex with his attractive intern Charlotte. Postcoitus and feeling a little more comfortable with Charlotte, as he's gotten to know her over the past few weeks, he comes to learn that her uncle was killed by a (presumably poorly driven) car many years ago. Congressman Bumblebrook immediately understands this to be a divine message. He realizes, then and there, that he has been given a mission: *America is plagued by pedestrian fatalities.* Clearly some higher power sees Ben Bumblebrook as the man with the answer. "I will not disappoint," he tells his higher power, "and forgive me for bungling the marital vow thingy."

Armed with his firm belief that the power of the government can right all wrongs, he begins his mission. He immediately takes Charlotte away from the abstinence research she'd been working on and has her focus on his new goal: *protecting America's at-risk pedestrians from the threat of automobiles.* But how does one do that? Elevated crosswalks? Sidewalk barriers? Air bag suits? Ten-mph speed limits? It's hard work coming up with a solution. Everything seems to have enormous drawbacks or expense.

Again, a moment of divine intervention would seem to confirm Ben Bumblebrook's purpose in life: A lobbyist comes calling, and wouldn't you know it? He's got the answer! Scott Raeib is one of several well-dressed, BlackBerry-equipped individuals who represent the interests of UltraMegaSuperCorp, a very large conglomerate with subconglomerates and little-bitty conglomerates under those. It just so happens that one of UltraMegaSuperCorp's subsidiaries makes large, hood-mounted devices that wail like a banshee when the car is in motion. Why not, Raeib suggests, mandate that all cars mount such a device as the UltraScreech on their hoods? The ear-piercing, headache-inducing wail is noticeable from one hundred feet, so naturally pedestrians will be alerted to approaching cars and take necessary action. American lives will be saved!

Excellent.

The congressman knows he could use some help—preferably from a more experienced member of Congress. One from across the aisle, as they say. And one from across the aisle in the other house of Congress would really get things rolling.

Fortunately Senator Martin Steigsmartin is the answer. He's a senior politician and he's in the other of the two parties. As luck would have it, he's in the pocket of the labor unions, and the Ultra-Screech factory is unionized. Increased demand means more jobs, more jobs means more union members, and more union members means more dues and thus a stronger union with more money to put into Senator Steigsmartin's politics.

The two lawmakers put together a bill, but hasty-like because time is short and Americans are being flattened at an alarming rate! We have to act! When the bill is finally introduced in Congress, the Protecting Our Pedestrians Everywhere and Sparing Our Drivers Act (POPE-SODA), also known as Bumblebrook-Steigsmartin, is a masterpiece of legislative planning. All that's needed are a few de-tails. And presumably some earmarks to win votes.

The campaign to win the hearts and minds of the people begins and our congressmen take to the airwaves and stay on message in speeches and interviews. This is an alarming epidemic, we are told, and this legislation is the antidote. They point to frightening sta-tistics provided to them (for free!) by Scott Raeib and the helpful folks at his lobbying firm. Will it prevent pedestrians from being killed, people ask? Sure it will, is the answer. Will it be expensive? No. And whatever it does cost would be a small price to pay if it saves a life.

Much of the media like the message (slow news cycle), and the terrible threat of automobiles comes to the forefront. Cars are dangerous, the American people are at risk, et cetera. All TV newscasts lead off with stories of anyone in the region who's been struck by a car, until every American citizen, man-woman-child, is absolutely traumatized to cross the street whether he's in New York, New York, or Middle of Nowhere, Iowa. Cars could be anywhere. Hiding. Waiting. Eager to pounce and claim another victim. No one is safe and no one will be safe until the government does something. Anything.

There are dissenting voices, sure. The car companies grumble—they fear the expense of modifying their car designs and adding a new feature—but their voices are drowned out because big corporations are understood to be evil. And it *won't* be expensive, Bumblebrook-Steigsmartin reminds us, because it's not projected to be expensive. And what if it saves a life and that person goes on to create the next Microsoft or Google? Well, it'll have paid for itself many times over.

Experts weigh in on the merits or troubles of devices that screech like banshees on cars. The noise might cause discomfort, some say. *Pshaw:* It makes us safer! In comment sections on the Internet, wars rage. POPE-SODA's detractors face an angry, spittle-laden onslaught of pro-screech, anti-spelling advocates: "WHAT part of saveing the childrin dont you unnerstand!!!!!" and "if it save's 1 life its worth it, dumass."

Meanwhile, back at the Capitol there are deals to be made: "I'll vote for your bill if you vote for mine" is one and "Well, I'd really like to be on that committee you chair, hint-hint" is another. Gradually the voices of dissent fall off: The congressman, who represents the district where the UltraScreech factory is located, has become a big fan. The insurance lobby, having figured out that they stand to benefit from a reduction in pedestrian fatalities, is throwing soirées in D.C. to make sure everyone they toss money at is on board.

Because of the mandate that all cars must be retrofitted with an UltraScreech, every body shop owner and car dealer from coast to coast sees the merit of the new law. The only ones truly outraged—classic car buffs—are a minority. Frankly, their umbrage doesn't matter that much. Their hobby doesn't have much of a lobby.

The tide in favor of the law swells: "How can you be against something that creates American jobs and saves American lives?" To be so suggests that you are—dare I say it?—un-American. POPE-SODA needs to be passed, and *now,* because lives are at stake and inaction is unacceptable. Deliberation will cost lives and jobs. America needs POPE-SODA!

POPE-SODA's biggest and loudest detractor, Senator Nathan Smetzling, continues to bring up concerns about cost, feasibility, impact. He and his efforts immediately fall to the wayside when he's caught leaving a ritzy hotel with a busty escort. Congressman Bumblebrook wastes no time getting in front of the cameras to denounce his opponent:

"We've seen Senator Smetzling's poor judgment with regard to his marriage—how can we trust his judgment on POPE-SODA?" he asks.

Dissent is dead.

The bill passes overwhelmingly to become an act—only ideological stalwarts objecting and a few noncommittal, timid types abstaining. With much fanfare the president signs POPE-SODA into law.

Congressmen and congresswomen behind him clap. Photographers take pictures. Now the law must be understood and enacted. And perhaps read in its entirety.

As that happens some "oversights" start to come to light. Because it's not clearly specified, POPE-SODA applies not just to cars and trucks but anything with wheels. The rusted-out pickup trucks that have been sitting on your neighbor's lawn for two decades must also be brought into compliance, as well as boat trailers. And sit-down lawn mowers. And wheelbarrows. Cost estimates must be revised for the changes and the reality of the economic situation, which is that due to various unplanned-for import tariffs and unforeseen supply-chain issues, et cetera and yadda-yadda, the UltraScreech is a little more than eight times more expensive to produce and install than had originally been anticipated. New cars will have approximately $1,200 added to their sticker price as a result of the modifications. That cost will be spread out over the length of the car loan, of course, so the pinch won't be felt as much as it will be for current car owners who'll have to cough up the cash. This can be addressed later with the proposed Screeching Hood Ornament Installation Relief Act, which would take money from . . . somewhere else to help subsidize the process of car screechification and ease the financial burden placed on the ever-diminishing middle class. But that's for later. And yes, there's the unfortunate issue of the earmark for the Cat Farm that Kentucky slipped in the bill at the eleventh hour. It's almost as upsetting as the $17 million that Senator Jason D. Bellweather set aside for the construction of the Senator Jason D. Bellweather Post Office in Tucson.

And what of cars coming into the country from Canada for a visit? That possibility did not escape the attention of the bill's authors. Foreign cars are welcome in the United States without the UltraScreech modification as long as their horn works and they honk it every four seconds.

Soon after enactment, every car and truck on the road emits a high-decibel, ear-piercing wail—shattering the nerves, eardrums and tranquility of anyone in a thousand-foot radius. Yes, it was originally thought that the Screech Zone would be limited to one hundred feet but that was based on faulty data (bad decimal).

In short order, automobile insurers raise their premiums in response to a dramatic spike in rear-end collisions: It seems a constant, jarring shriek can be distracting for otherwise capable drivers, not to mention there are Canadians all over the place honking their horns every four seconds. It's very unnerving.

Dead animals with pained expressions frozen on their faces and blood trickling from their ears begin to line the highways and busy roads of the entire country. It's too early to determine what's causing this, Bumblebrook-Steigsmartin supporters remind us. Studies must be done. Any theories as to the extraordinary circumstances of the animals' demise and any suggestion that their end might be related to enactment of POPE-SODA will have to wait. There are far more pressing issues anyway—such as the rapid rise of childhood deafness, panic attacks and chronic insomnia in America's urban centers. To name a few.

Recriminations start to trickle in. The authors of Bumblebrook-Steigsmartin find themselves a little bit on the defensive. It's too soon to make judgments, they tell us. You have to give these things time. And after all, it is saving lives, isn't it? Statistics by the National Highway Traffic Safety Administration point toward yes. Briefly, anyway. After a dramatic decline things seem to have reached a plateau—presumably as pedestrians began shoving wads of cotton in their ears, or just got used to the shrill, nerve-racking sound emitted by every passing automobile. And motorcycle. And bike. And people on Rollerblades (another oversight in the original bill's language).

Not too long into things there's not a single Canadian car in the country, and studies indicate a toll booth worker takes his or her life every nineteen minutes. An increasing number of Americans start to have second thoughts about their support for POPE-SODA. On television shows, accosted by pundits and reporters, members of Congress who raved about POPE-SODA and cheered it into existence adamantly deny ever raving about the law. They drop lines like "We couldn't have known" and "I was misled" and "It was the right thing to do at the time." They're adamant that we understand they were against it before they supported it.

But the law still has its friends and supporters. Yes, it makes our lives execrable but it saves them, maybe. UltraMegaSuperCorp has seen unprecedented profits and its Chinese shareholders are tickled pink. Trade unions have reaped great rewards with their new members happily paying their dues. Automobile insurers might just buy a skyscraper or two. Maybe naming rights to a stadium! Ear doctors have had business increase tenfold, according to an industry survey. They now have their own lobby pushing for POPE-SODA to apply to watercraft and aircraft as well. The manufacturers of cotton, earplugs, headphones, alcohol, sleep aids, anxiety medication and antidepressants are all incredibly happy.

So POPE-SODA, despite its minor faults and regardless of its cost-to-benefit ratio, won't be going anywhere anytime soon. Bumblebrook-Steigsmartin have their law, have made their mark. They're certainly not going to risk upsetting their biggest donors.

In the meantime, Congress has other fish to fry, other laws to conceive, throw together and get passed. Perhaps they'll address making some revisions to Bumblebrook-Steigsmartin in the next session if there's time.

Mission Accom—oh, never mind.

10

OUR POLITICIANS

On second thought, don't take me to your leader

Mothers all want their sons to grow up to be president, but
they don't want them to become politicians in the process.

—JOHN F. KENNEDY

$\mathfrak{The}$ United States pooh-poohed the concept of monarchy, and had plenty of good reasons for doing so, but that does not at all mean they wanted just anyone running the place. Far from it. Running a country isn't just like raising a child—where you can simply hire the first nanny who responds to your ad on Craigslist, hand your baby over and get on with your life. This is important! The Founders and their close friends, and those who clung to the Founders like teens on a Bieber, certainly believed there was such a thing as a "ruling class" that was composed of learned men with nicer shoes, wigs and pants than the other folks. The existence of the Electoral College and the fact that originally senators were chosen by state legislatures, not you, serve as testament to that fact. So, government by the people, sure, for the people, indeed—just not any people. And that's fine, really, because when you wander through any supermarket you can mostly point to people you would not want running the show, especially one of the Greater Shows on Earth.

What was particularly lovely about the American system was that unlike a stuffy old monarchy, where you had to be the lucky duck who was born into power, you could actually break into the business of running the American Republic if you tried hard enough. Granted, it was much easier if you had some land and money, but that's always been the way now, hasn't it?

At the beginning, politics was essentially well-to-do white guys. Further down the timeline they were joined by moderately-to-do white guys. Eventually they were joined by white guys who were able to overcome the obstacle of not being particularly to-do. And then, in 1870—a black guy. Hiram Rhodes Revels was elected as senator—representing the great state of Mississippi. Before you go thinking that Mississippi must have been some amazingly progressive state, bear in mind that these were the days before the Seventeenth Amendment, when senators were chosen by state legislators. Had the people of Mississippi been directly involved with the vote, Revels might have had a tougher go of it. As it was, his election faced fierce opposition from . . . Democrats.

I understand perfectly if the idea of a black Republican being elected senator in Mississippi over the protests of white Democrats is messing with you. Might be a good moment to step outside and get some air.

Of course, opening the doors of Congress to a black guy naturally set a precedent: *Congress isn't just for white guys!* Slippery slope that was, and much to the consternation of many, no doubt, Congress wound up with its very first female *forty-six years later.* Jeannette

Rankin of Montana entered the House of Representatives in 1916 and naturally, in the bizarro world of yesteryear's politics, she was a Republican who hated war and helped create the ACLU.

It's true—you can't make this stuff up.

What American history has shown us is that it is possible, technically, for most anyone to enter the world of politics. Yes, it helps to be rich and yes, it helps to be white, but in that sense it's no different than Wall Street or *Us Weekly*. The fact of the matter is that when we call ourselves the "Land of Opportunity" it's not complete bunkum like "Best Happy Hour in Town" or "Lowest Prices," because we actually mean it.

That accessibility has given us a great menagerie of interesting characters who have made their mark on American political history. For many of them it was a mark they weren't actually too keen to make but make it they did.

The concept of the "public servant" is a noble one indeed, and at the time it came into being—a time long before electricity, reality television or Viagra—it referred to an individual who was so selfless he was willing to take time away from his family, farm and business to head to the nation's capital and contribute to the governance of the land. It didn't pay that well and, given the fact that you had to haul yourself to the capital by horse over crap roads and stay there while Congress was in session, it was a serious pain in the ass (literally, too, due to the aforementioned horse and crap roads). It was a significant expenditure of time in an era when forty-year-olds were considered senior citizens. Overall, you could be forgiven for not being so enthusiastic about serving the public and hoping that someone else might be more inclined to step in, so that you might tend to your crops and spend quality time with your wife in case she died in childbirth, as was the fashion.

Those who did serve their public did so because they felt it was a duty. Being able to participate in government was also a delightful novelty for people who only recently had left England, a country with such an entrenched hierarchy that your entire life trajectory was determined solely by the answer to *Who's your daddy?*

America dispensed with all the pretentious traditions of nobility. There would be no king shouting about his Divine Right to tell you what to do. There were no barons or viscounts, no princes or earls. One William might be rich and another William might be poor, but they were both just William. A William was a William and never a Lord William would he be. That was good news for the poor William, as he would not have to suffer the indignity of rich William prancing around, calling himself fancy names. And in addition to not having a Lord William lording over him, the poor William was lucky to live in a land of opportunity (and Indians—but they were slowly taking care of that). He might someday become a rich William himself! Even so, he'd still be just William because this is America and in America nobody cares about titles. The only nobility we recognize is that of the A-list Hollywood celebrity and the occasional classless, stupid, slutty granddaughter of late hotel chain magnates.

It's only natural that a country founded with liberty in mind, with an enormous expanse of land to the west and a gullible Indian population, would grow. And grow it did. But as the country grew so did the country's government. The business of being a public servant became more of a business.

These days being a public servant isn't just a hobby. You don't put down your hoe and head to Washington to help out for a stretch. Over the course of our nearly 250 years, we've grown from a noble experiment in governance "By the People, for the People" into the dominant force on the world stage. We have bested the Yahoos and AltaVistas. We are the Google of nations! (In all honesty, I was drawn to this analogy because Google's competitor, Bing, sounds Chinese.)

Our unprecedented success has over time, and especially in recent history, built itself into an absolutely enormous government filled with people who've been drawn to it for a multitude of reasons. Like moths to a flame (and many of them do in fact get burned). There are patriots and pirates, statesmen and sleazeballs, imbeciles and rocket scientists (literally: New Jersey congressman Rush Holt, Jr., can safely put "rocket scientist" on his résumé).

Everyone in Congress from the lowliest freshmen to the headline-dominating titans is a public servant, though We the Public seem to have to remind them of this fact on a fairly regular basis. These days many of our public servants have priorities, with the public not always ranking at number one. As a result, our nation's political class enjoys a trust and favorability ranking somewhere in the neighborhood of auto mechanics and the guy who charged me three hundred dollars to not fix my fridge.

Since the United States has been in business, the cast of characters that has passed through Congress has been varied and diverse—especially after we started letting minorities and women play too. The people who have roamed the halls of the Capitol Building have ranged from the privileged sons of the country's dynasties, to the people who stumbled into things, to the inspiring rags-to-riches types.

Their achievements have ranged dramatically from doing pretty much nothing to creating laws that will continue to plague future generations.

The following politicians are merely a sampling of the many,

many memorable individuals who have roamed the halls of Congress:

THE FORTUNATE SON

Would seemingly troubled drug and whore enthusiast Charlie Sheen have been able to make it in Hollywood if he weren't the son of A-list Hollywood actor Martin Sheen? Or would he have been just another seemingly troubled drug and whore enthusiast trying to make it in Tinseltown? Unfortunately we'll never know. Martin Sheen is his dad, and there's nothing we can do about that.

There's no shortage of actors in Hollywood who have benefited from their familial connections. I vaguely recall reading that Tori Spelling claimed she'd given casting directors an alias when she auditioned for her father Aaron Spelling's *Beverly Hills 90210*. The suggestion being that her landing the role had nothing to do with her paternal connections. I vaguely remember laughing very, very much at that notion.

We can't fault anyone for wanting to get their children in on a lucrative profession. If I had a swell one, I'd certainly prop open the door for my children—if it's what they wanted to do—and give them some pointers, make some introductions, give them lead roles in my movie. Whatever it takes. If they later suffered self-doubt about their innate abilities, and that led them to be troubled drug and whore enthusiasts? Well, that's unfortunate but at least they wouldn't be hitting me up for money when I'm eighty.

Just like the Hustons, Curtises, Redgraves, Barrymores, Fondas, Carradines, Douglases and Coppolas, Washington has its very own fortunate sons and daughters for whom barriers have been lowered, doors have been flung open, seats have been kept warm and who in general have benefited greatly from connections that you and I could only dream of. How much easier things might be for us were we the son or daughter of an Adams, Bush, Taft, Roosevelt, Long, Gore, Dailey, Rockefeller and of course, Kennedy.

TED KENNEDY told *60 Minutes,* shortly before his death, that going into politics wasn't much of an option for him. His dad's "get in or get lost" ultimatum prompted Kennedy to enter public service just like his older brothers John and Robert had done. Thus began a career that would span nearly a half century and make him one of the most powerful members of Congress.

Edward's background will seem familiar to any student of dynastic politics: He was born into great wealth. His school grades were mediocre but he got into Harvard anyway. He got expelled from Harvard for cheating. He joined the U.S. Army for the minimal two years and spent the Korean War safely hunkered down in Paris, France. After discharge he reentered Harvard (they're very forgiving) and followed up with a stint at the University of Virginia Law School, from which he graduated in 1959. Three years later he was a U.S. senator. Not too shabby!

The biggest test of Kennedy's political career came in 1969, when the car he was driving—at night, after a party—sailed off a bridge on Chappaquiddick Island. Kennedy, by now a young, married senator, escaped unharmed but his passenger, twenty-eight-year-old Mary Jo Kopechne, drowned.

This terrible incident served to separate the political wheat from the chaff, as it were. A mere mortal who wasn't contemplating his Senate career and a future presidency would have likely run, screaming, for help. But Kennedy, presumably terrified that his prospects were going up in smoke/down in water, ran home to consult with family and lawyers, and reported the incident in the morning. Thanks to the water that his car rested in, his baptism as a true politician was complete.

As will happen when sons and daughters of the elite suffer terrible scandal, Kennedy apologized and received a slap on the wrist. The inquest was sealed, indictments never materialized and the matter was shelved. A cottage industry of books regarding the incident followed soon after. A forgiving Massachusetts public reelected him to the Senate by a large margin the following year.

The conventional wisdom of the time said that any presidential aspirations Kennedy may have had were effectively dashed on the rocks, and indeed when Kennedy tried to seize the Democratic nomination from the unpopular Jimmy Carter in 1980, the incident resurfaced many times. Yes, pun intended. Ultimately Kennedy failed to take the nomination from Carter, but is considered to have contributed greatly to weakening Carter—who then went on to lose against Ronald Reagan.

Let Ted Kennedy serve as a lesson to this nation's politically minded privileged class: An act of youthful negligence resulting in a fatality could very well keep you from achieving the highest office in the land, and instead relegate you to merely being one of the most powerful and influential senators in the history of the United States.

THE WAR VETERAN

Americans are very proud of their military and have been ever since *Born on the Fourth of July* made us all feel bad about harassing and abusing our Vietnam veterans. We go out of our way to let the men and women of the armed services know we love them. We buy them drinks and put ribbons on our cars to let them know we support them. When, during Fleet Week in New York City, we find them facedown on the sidewalk outside our apartment, we give them cab fare so they can get back to their ship before curfew. We make sure if we say, "The Iraq War is a mistake," that we then tack on, "But I support our troops." Just in case there's any doubt. We love our military. There's a reason so many beggars pretend that they're veterans.

Our politicians love the military too. The surefire way to get a crowd riled up is to invoke the soldiers. The music business equivalent is "Are you ready to rock?" to which everyone roars. In politics you say, "The men and women of our armed services!" and everyone cheers.

Our politicians also love the military because having it on their résumé makes them look like good, America-loving patriots. If you have two otherwise absolutely identical candidates running for office, A and B, but B was in the Marine Corps, B's the winner. It's exactly like two identical girls with fantastic personalities, but B has bigger boobs. B's the winner. Don't believe the "empowering" ladies' magazines that say otherwise.

Some politicians simply serve their country without overthinking their future political strategy. Veterans such as John McCain, John F. Kennedy, Bob Dole, John Kerry, George McGovern or George H. W. Bush actually did find themselves in harm's way. Later, they were able to cash in on their military street cred when on the campaign trail.

Other aspiring political stars who recognized the value of military service on the résumé seem to have spent a lot of time figuring out how they can serve their country without being in the uncomfortable position of being shot at. Through luck or political machination they found themselves manning the back lines during periods of conflict or showing up three days late to a firefight. For some, as memory fades or their desire to be elected grows, their military service record blossoms. Deferments and medical leaves are forgotten, sitting at a desk is mistaken for a hot zone and guarding a latrine becomes a national security operation. Connecticut governor Dick Blumenthal, Illinois senator Mark Kirk, George W. Bush and yes, conservative hero Ronald Reagan have all suffered from fabricating or embellishing their service records. The technical term for this is "misremembering." Some are much better at misremembering than others.

To hear DOUGLAS R. STRINGFELLOW describe it, he enjoyed an impeccable military background. He was a decorated Army Air Force hero of the Second World War. As an agent in the OSS, predecessor to today's CIA, he participated in top secret missions, as secret agents will do. After being captured by the Germans he was held in the notorious Belsen prison and ruthlessly tortured until he was rendered a paraplegic. Eventually he was able to escape from the Nazis and make his way back home. He received a well-deserved Silver Star for his troubles. Once safely on home soil he decided to run for office. The soldier-adoring population of Utah was more than happy to overwhelmingly elect him to represent them in the House of Representatives in 1952.

Two years later, as happens to all representatives per the Constitution, Stringfellow found himself running for reelection. Unfortunately, Stringfellow's opponent was not as smitten by his war hero record. Or, perhaps he was smitten, but regardless of how smitten he may have been he thought it might be prudent to make an attempt to verify its *truthiness*.

What they came to learn was a political campaign's dream. The Mother of All Discoveries. Greater than finding Bill Clinton's blue dress wrapped around the John Edwards love child in a room at the Watergate Hotel: Robert Stringfellow's claims were complete and utter bullshit. There were no OSS exploits because he hadn't been in the OSS. He was not captured by the Germans and therefore had no prison from which to escape from. Since he wasn't a POW, he also wasn't tortured. And since he wasn't tortured, well, you guessed it: not a paraplegic either. And the Silver Star perhaps existed in a parallel universe where Kim Kardashian was Einstein and potatoes were rectangles—but not this universe. Stringfellow, a private in the Army Air Force, did have a limp due to an unfortunate—albeit, not uncommon—encounter with a land mine.

Oh, and for added *oomph* his Democratic opponent checked in with the colleges Stringfellow said he had attended. As you can imagine, they'd never heard of him.

It matters not whether *misremember* was a word back in 1954. There's really no way to misremember so many things, however hard one may try. Stringfellow bid adieu to politics immediately, withdrew from the race, and did the only thing you can really do after that—limped off and died in obscurity.

I take that back. He did the only thing you could do *back then*. These days he'd have his own TV show à la Eliot Spitzer.

THE LOON

Crazy people are a fact of life. You come to understand this quickly in a big city, especially one where you're on foot and not safely cocooned in an automobile. They rant and rave and shake their fists at invisible antagonists. They shuffle around in soiled pants, or no pants, stare at you, yell at you and often cause you to divert your course—just to be safe. Sometimes the insanity takes a milder form—obsessing over a celebrity, hoarding cats or shooting off angry, rambling emails to newspapers.

Most of us feel sympathy for individuals who've fallen a few cigarettes short of a pack. Instead of reacting angrily as they tell a packed subway car that women are demons, we just look away, or we give them money or even try to get them help. Sometimes we elect them to office.

CYNTHIA McKINNEY has the honor of being the first black woman to represent the state of Georgia after her 1992 election to the House of Representatives. That would have been more of an accomplishment had she not been elected by the highly gerrymandered Eleventh District that was 64 percent black and very, very Democratic. Nevertheless, as we've transcended race, she will likely be remembered for her other accomplishments: Accusing George W. Bush of complicity in the September 11 attacks, accusing the CIA of having a hand in assassinating Martin Luther King, Jr., and rapper Tupac Shakur and accusing Al Gore of having a low "Negro tolerance level" even though his campaign manager, Donna Brazile, was black. McKinney was also known for her dislike of Israel, support for Palestine and penning an obsequious open love letter to Saudi Prince Alwaleed bin Talal after his $10 million donation was snubbed by New York mayor Rudy Giuliani following the 9/11 attacks. Her bodyguards of choice were the New Black Panther Party, known for being a little bit racist, a little bit anti-Semitic and a lot bit crazy.

McKinney ultimately found herself defeated in the 2002 primary for any of the above stated reasons. In an effort to motivate any fence-sitters the night before the primary, her father appeared on Atlanta television to let folks know "Jews have bought everybody. J-E-W-S."

But, wait, she wasn't finished!

McKinney (amazingly) found herself back in Congress in 2005, eager to pick up where she'd left off. She resumed her 9/11 conspiracy agenda and went on to introduce Articles of Impeachment against George W. Bush, Dick Cheney and (lest she be accused of racism) Condoleezza Rice.

The congresswoman's pièce de résistance was assaulting a Capitol Hill police officer who'd stopped her to ask for identification. Although McKinney had changed her hairstyle and was not wearing her congressional pin, she blamed the incident on racial profiling. This time, however, she was unable to drum up any significant defense from her own party. Even Al Sharpton.

If Al Sharpton isn't even willing to defend you, you know you're in trouble.

After being questioned about the incident by a reporter, McKinney unwittingly (is there any other way, really?) made embarrassing comments that were picked up by a nearby microphone. Realizing this, she then returned to instruct reporters that they were not allowed to use any audio that was recorded *when she was not seated*. Reporters, savvy as they are, realized there was no such law on the books and the unfortunate audio aired nationally in short order.

Being loopy, punching policemen and saying stupid things took its toll on her constituency.

McKinney was ultimately knocked out of the 2006 primary by Hank Johnson, who went on to handily win the seat and establish a legacy of his own. During a House Armed Services Committee hearing, Johnson worried that putting too many U.S. troops on Guam might cause the island to "tip over and capsize."

Presumably this district would be a great place to open a

chiropractic office, as the residents must have their necks out of alignment from shaking their heads all the time.

THE HYPOCRITE

Americans love themselves some good comeuppance. There's just so much joy to be had in watching hypocrisy unveiled and seeing the once proud and pious, finger-wagging holier-than-thous trip and fall from the rooftops of their poorly constructed glass houses.

When someone bad-mouths gays we don't give them too much attention. But when they bad-mouth gays, say gays are evil deviants, say gays are destroying the country, fight for anti-gay legislation—and then that same someone is found sodomizing one of America's evil, deviant, America-destroying gays—well, it honestly doesn't get much better than that.

As a country we take immeasurable delight in witnessing the rapid descent-into-fireball of the mistress-juggling champion of marriage and family values. We cheer when the children of abstinence advocates get knocked up. We rejoice when anti-immigration flag-bearers suddenly find themselves having to explain why an illegal Mexican is holding their laundry basket. And we cry with joy when anti-prostitution crusaders get caught red-handed and barepenised.

Every time it happens, and it happens a lot, we wonder to ourselves, *Why?* Why would someone conduct themselves in such a way that, when their absurd hypocrisy is ultimately revealed, people would have cause to jump for joy at intensity levels not seen since toothless, illiterate women in Gaza cheered the fall of the twin towers.

During the saga we'll call *The Adventures of Bill Clinton,* advocates for the impeachment of the philandering cad were plenty. Some of the most vocal included Newt Gingrich, Henry Hyde, Bob Barr, Dan Burton, Helen Chenoweth-Hage, Bob Livingston and others who were so outraged by Clinton's behavior that they apparently forgot they'd *all* cheated on their spouses too.

Most of us can relate to hypocrisy, since we are hypocrites in varying degrees. We tell people how to save money but ignore our own advice. We rail against the government while our fat asses droop over the seat of our Medicare-acquired mobility scooter. We curse at people driving the exact same way we drive. And we grimace and sneer at children on planes because our own kids are at home. But hypocritical as we are, we're not stupid about it—most of us. We don't set ourselves up for colossal levels of embarrassment and humiliation by telling the world how bad it is to be doing something we actually are doing. This, apparently, is what differentiates us from a lot of politicians.

TED KLAUDT served the public through the South Dakota House of Representatives from 1999 to 2006. During his career, the good citizens of South Dakota came to understand two things: He was grotesquely fat, and he deeply disliked sex offenders.

I know you know where this is going, but bear with me.

During his tenure he introduced and cosponsored several pieces of legislation aimed at making the lives of sex offenders difficult. He worked tirelessly to add his state to the National Sex Offender Registry. NSOR is an online database of sex offenders that includes everyone from bona fide rapists to seventeen-year-old guys who slept with their sixteen-year-old girlfriends and have had their lives ruined as a result. So it needs a little work, but I digress.

The sex offender laws Klaudt pushed were the usual fare. They barred offenders from living or being within five hundred feet of schools, public pools and parks. They defined what was considered a "sex crime" and the process for having sex offenders register in the state. And they created a state sex offender website.

Naturally, you would come to expect that a politician as nobly engaged in protecting the children would be found guilty of raping his foster children. And so he was. Two girls. Four counts. Forty-four years in prison. Plus two convictions for witness tampering.

Many of our nation's great political hypocrites, once they are shamed beyond belief, simply choose to disappear and live out their lives quietly somewhere. Presumably with their heads hung low. Very understandable. The case of Ted Klaudt, however, is different. You would presume he'd live his life out in prison, which he doesn't really have a choice about at this point. But no. Having been horribly shamed by raping the girls he had been entrusted with, he tried to clear his name.

By—literally—clearing his name.

From prison, Klaudt issued notice to news organizations that his name had been copyrighted and could not be used without his consent. Legal opinion disagreed with Klaudt's attempt to set a stupid precedent and as a result you can safely mention Ted Klaudt without his permission, or the fear of being sued. In fact, Klaudt's clumsy effort to clear his name clearly backfired as it cast a national spotlight on what would have simply been your run-of-the-mill, sex-law-advocating, morbidly obese child rapist.

THE SCOUNDREL

By now we've all heard some variation of Lord Acton's famous "Power tends to corrupt" quotation half a billion times. The reason we keep hearing it is, of course, because it has been true since time immemorial. Lord Acton pointing it out didn't change anything—people in power continued to enjoy the fruits of corruption but his quote gave us a much more eloquent way to call them out than simply screaming, "Those SOBs are crooks!"

Celebrities, when confronted with bad press, check into "rehab." When confronted with egregious malfeasance, our nation's elite take a different tack: They are immediately transformed from ruthless, motivated power players into hapless, bumbling, apologetic saps. Even the most seasoned of them "didn't realize," "misunderstood," and "had no knowledge of" the transgressions for which they are being accused. At once they are naive souls, wholly incapable of connecting any dots or totally capable of insisting that the dots don't even exist to connect: "SuperMegaCorp allowed me use of their private plane, and tropical island resort, and paid for my daughter's wedding, and honeymoon—but that had *absolutely nothing* to do with my helping them get their bill passed."

Their seemingly childlike innocence prevents them not only from drawing the obvious conclusions that the rest of us do, but also from comprehending the very world they live in. They seem genuinely surprised to discover that laws against what they are doing actually exist. Not only that, but that often they themselves had a hand in creating those very laws. Once again they "didn't realize," "misunderstood," "had no knowledge of" anything. And they're always terribly, terribly sorry.

What's impressive is that despite their self-proclaimed inability to see the forest for the trees, or to put two and two together, or to understand the basic laws of the land they govern, they're always able to summon the Machiavellian shrewdness, savvy and cunning necessary for getting themselves elected to office when the time comes.

CHARLIE RANGEL, representative from New York, epitomizes the career politician who, during his forty years as a "public servant," has worked his way into Washington, like a tick into your scalp.

Rangel, who'd been awarded a Bronze Star and Purple Heart in the Korean War, who'd worked as a lawyer in his native Harlem and who worked hard on behalf of his impoverished district, could easily serve as poster child for the power of Congress to corrupt individuals of impressive stock. He'll now be remembered as the power-abusing, hubristic, hypocritical scoundrel he's become. One so thoroughly used to the perks of power that he cannot comprehend things going any way but the way he wants them to. Perfect example: He expected his November 2010 ethics hearing to be postponed when he showed up without lawyers, despite having had two years to prepare. The movement to postpone was denied and Rangel, utterly stunned at that fact, simply left. Make sure to try that the next time you're in traffic court and see how that pans out. *Your Honor, I didn't think you guys were serious.*

What wound up bringing Congressman Rangel into an ethics hearing in the first place was quintessential political corruption: a history of acceptance of illegal gifts, a history of taking advantage of the position and a history of "forgetting" to report income. That the chair of the powerful *tax code writing* Ways and Means Committee can't remember how to pay taxes is alarming and enraging enough. Couple that deficiency with numerous other overtly shady deeds and you can understand why in 2009, Citizens for Responsibility and Ethics in Washington named Rangel one of the fifteen most corrupt members of Congress.

His censure was a start. It's certainly not enough. And Rangel, like Gollum in *Lord of the Rings,* simply has no understanding of what it is he's become.

THE IMPLODER

Once, not too long ago, my friend Joe turned to me in the back of a cab in New York and, tearing up, told me his life was perfect. Wife, child and career all on track. And he was terrified. At that moment I realized the truth: Give someone a great spouse, wonderful children and a generally happy life and you essentially provide them with a lingering sense of dread, a haunting fear that something terrible could happen at a moment's notice and ruin everything they have. A brain tumor, murderous burglar, heart attack, drunk driver, plummeting stock market—you name it, and they're spending their happy times bracing for it.

For politicians it's no better. They know full well that their moments in the sun could, within seconds, be cast into total darkness by clouds extending well beyond the horizon. The wrong sound bite, a bad photo op, skeletons freeing themselves from closets—any politician worth noting is surrounded by hundreds of ticking time bombs and knows that there are plenty of people who would likely cheer their detonation. All their glory is tempered by the knowledge that their political fortunes could come crashing down twice as fast as they had risen.

The American public is fickle, terribly so, and even the most seemingly trivial items have the power to sail into the sky, fly right up your tailpipe, explode and send your whole mess crashing down to the ground. Case in point: Dukakis in a tank hat.

You see, Democrats are viewed by a large segment of the American population as being lightweights on military issues. This seems to be the result of good Republican PR rather than actual reality. We entered World War I, World War II, Korea and Vietnam with a Democrat president at the helm. Nevertheless, many Americans see the Democrats as pathetic milquetoasts who wouldn't raise a finger to defend the country and whose timidity and lack of resolve to use force places us all in danger. By virtue of having been actually shot out of the sky during World War II, Dukakis's opponent, George Herbert Walker Bush, had an edge when it came to military credits. The Dukakis campaign, knowing this and sensing that their candidate needed some, decided that the best way to bolster the image of Mike Dukakis as Warrior President was to put a helmet on him and plunk him into a tank.

If you've never had the pleasure of seeing the image for yourself, allow me to describe it for you: a diminutive man with a unibrow and a forced smile wearing a helmet six sizes too big addressing the camera with a big thumbs-up. In no time the Dukakis campaign's wings had fallen off, and it began its rapid descent toward the unforgiving earth.

While some implosions are smallish affairs others are fantastic, glorious supernovas that bathe us in a majestic light and a hell of a lot of entertainment before compacting into cold, dead stars. John Edwards was one of the more recent examples of this phenomenon. First rising to stardom as the VP choice in John Kerry's failed 2004 run for the presidency, he'd been bitten by the bug. In 2008 he was back again, hoping to clinch the nomination from its presumed heir, Hillary Clinton. And then came the reports of the affair. And the denial. And the baby. And the denial. And begging his campaign manager to take the fall. And the acknowledgment of the affair, but denial of the baby. And, despite being incredibly damaged goods, his insistence on offering himself as VP candidate. Then the acceptance of the baby. It was delightful. But it still wasn't among the best.

JOSEPH McCARTHY, who looked a little like Pat Buchanan, achieved such notoriety that he joins the likes of Darwin, Kafka, Machiavelli, Freud and Jacuzzi whose names have entered the lexicon and become nouns, verbs and adjectives. Unfortunately, in McCarthy's case *McCarthyism* means being a complete bastard whom everyone eventually comes to hate.

In the early years of the Cold War, long before most folks came to realize that the Soviet system was stupid and untenable, everyone was terrified of commies. Not only had they recently acquired nuclear weaponry, but they were masters of infiltration. Friends, relatives, neighbors, in fact just about anyone could potentially be a communist sympathizer or agent. Just as in *Invasion of the Body Snatchers* no one knew whom they could trust. They needed a person to scream and point at someone, so they could all start screaming and pointing too.

The senator from Wisconsin saw potential here. The American people were frightened. Commies were potentially everywhere. He was going to help us root them out. Beginning in 1950, McCarthy, wholly unburdened with facts and willing to accept hearsay as truth, began his jihad and started shouting about the enemy within. His first target was the Democrat Truman's State Department. In response, televised hearings were called. Democrats had hoped to take advantage of the hearings to embarrass McCarthy and shut him up. Instead, and in all too typical Democratic fashion, they shot themselves in the foot. With the cameras on him and the country engrossed, the firebrand upped the ante and the rhetoric even more, charging individuals by name and continuing his Big Parade of Evidence-Free Accusations. It made for some good TV. The public was galvanized, the Congress was polarized and McCarthy was officially a star. Naturally the committee was split among partisan lines. The Republicans saw a problem, the Democrats didn't, which led the Republicans to shout "treason!" and "conspiracy!" with wild abandon.

With a hungry audience and a reputation to maintain, McCarthy had to lower his standards for what exactly a "communist" was. The fires had to be fanned and there was no time to tone down the hysteria. Political opponents were labeled as sympathizers or accused of protecting traitors. In the style of Reuters they released doctored photographs—ironically, a very Soviet thing to do—suggesting certain politicians were cavorting with communists.

The Republicans fared well in the 1950 election, and McCarthy was widely credited for many of those gains. A Catholic himself, McCarthy developed a large fan base of Catholic Democrats. In short order he was not only welcomed by the Kennedy clan, but dating within it and eventually godfather to Robert F. Kennedy's first child. This Kennedy-McCarthy love fest should be seen for what it likely really was: the Democrat and terribly clever Joseph Kennedy hoping that the rising Republican star McCarthy would pave the way for his Catholic sons in Congress. Politics is politics, people.

With the election of Dwight D. Eisenhower in 1952, McCarthy finally had the Republican boss he'd always wanted. Many people had been kicked to the curb, based in most cases on little to no evidence—and that was with a hostile Truman administration. Imagine the field day he could have with a friendly one! Alas, it didn't take long for the McCarthy-Eisenhower marriage to move from one of convenience to estrangement to open hostility. A furious McCarthy—still convinced commies were everywhere—stormed up and down the Senate aisles, eager for a showdown with the president. However, a savvy Eisenhower refused to grace him with more national exposure.

By 1953 the fire was out of control. McCarthy's subcommittee grilled suspects in front of cameras, obliterated careers with merely an accusation and pushed libraries to destroy subversive literature. Having bulldozed through one entity after another on his Commie Quest, McCarthy soon focused his super-pinko-X-ray-vision on the U.S. Army.

In doing so, he helped turn the tide against himself by prompting what is arguably the most famous quote from all the hearings, delivered by U.S. Army counsel Joseph Welch: "Have you no sense of decency, sir? At long last, have you left no sense of decency?"

People cheered. McCarthy had officially jumped the shark. His public popularity was on the decline. Media legends like Edward R. Murrow tore him to shreds with the kind of eloquence sorely lacking in journalism these days. By late 1954 he had been censured (of course, not by John F. Kennedy, who missed the vote) and would remain largely shunned by his colleagues in the Senate.

In less than three years he drank himself to death and everyone lived happily ever after.

THE GHOST OF POLITICIANS FUTURE

With an election on the way (there's always an election on the way) we're sure to be introduced to some intriguing and exciting new characters, or have some old ones taken down from the shelf, dusted off and repackaged for us. Not as the politicians that they were but the politicians that they will be. To hear Gingrich bandied about as a 2012 contender after a decade in hibernation has to have taken more than a few people by surprise. It just goes to show that old politicians never die; they just remain in stasis—issuing the occasional op-ed and writing the occasional book—until the right opportunity comes along.

11

The Campaign Trail

The never-ending story

Campaign season, like Christmas season, seems to start earlier and earlier every year. Campaign 2012 began in earnest about ten minutes after the 2010 midterm polls closed. I'm sure you were thrilled about that, as we all were.

Like Christmas, Campaign-mas season often comes with scads of presents. But instead of flimsy, disposable toys produced with toxic chemicals in China we get presents for grown-ups—in the form of preposterous statements, disastrous candidates and self-destructing campaigns. Every day in the months leading up to an election we get to unwrap a delightful new gift. A photo of a candidate sucking on a dildo at a party, for example, or a revelation that someone wasn't wholly truthful in their dealings with the Department of Revenue. Perhaps they had an illegal alien mowing their estate—as they stood on the sidelines dressed as a Nazi (just reenacting, people!). Hints of mistresses, hookers and illegitimate children. Embarrassing appearances on TV shows of yesteryear, embellished military records. Allegations, revelations, denials—it's all nothing short of delightful watching candidates squirm and grimace, backpedal and weep under the harsh light of scrutiny and gaze of an occasionally noncomplacent media.

Unless of course they're picking on *our* candidate, in which case we'll make excuse upon excuse to defend him or her. The more partisan among us are fully capable of rising to the highest levels of absolute comic absurdity in the defense of the blatantly obvious. Sometimes it's so bad we reach the point where we expect Rod Serling himself to step out of the shadows at any moment and explain the dynamics of the twilight zone we've currently entered.

It is under these circumstances that we watch helplessly as mobs proceed to attack the journalist who dared ask a candidate what newspapers she read. The answer was clearly "None," but in the case of *Couric v. Palin* that didn't matter to the tireless defenders of Mama Grizzly; her backers instead reacted angrily to her abysmal performance on that question (and several others) as though the obviously hostile journalist had demanded an immediate and accurate answer to some unknowable mathematical equation. Couric certainly had posed a gotcha question, and there's no doubt it was meant to bring to light what many journalists knew and what much of the population suspected: that Lady Sarah is not too keen on current events.

"She was just trying to make her look bad" was the general tone of the lamentation. Well, yes, Couric was and, yes, Palin did. But only kind of, because there was no shortage of people who took umbrage that such a question was posed in the first place. Really? Seemed fairly straightforward.

Frankly, compared to Mike Dukakis being asked if he'd support the death penalty should his wife be raped and murdered, I think she got off pretty easy. Unlike Palin, Dukakis answered honestly (a firm "No" in his trademark charmless manner) and paid dearly for it.

Naturally, the loser in this story turned out not to be Palin but Couric herself—vilified on TV, radio, in weblogs and comment sections throughout cyberspace for having the audacity to ask such a mundane question of someone seeking to be a heartbeat away from the presidency. Was it catty? Yes. Should someone seeking the vice presidency read newspapers? Yes.

The 2010 midterms have their own greatest hits. The one good thing to come from revelations that Connecticut U.S. senator Dick Blumenthal repeatedly lied about his service in Vietnam was that he probably won't be able to lie about it anymore. Or, to use the political vernacular: He won't be able to *misspeak* anymore. His campaign suffered a brief moment of discomfort, a fart in a spacesuit, but Dick was able to overcome his troubles by taking us on a journey to a special world where green is blue and up is down. In the spirit of "I am not a crook" and "I did not have sex with that woman," we learned that telling audiences that you served in Vietnam—several times—was an "unintentional and rare misstatement." In fact, we came to learn, Senator Blumenthal was actually hoping he would be called into service, despite the fact that every step he took back then—five deferments and joining the Marine Corps Reserve—worked to avoid that reality coming to pass. War Hero Blumenthal ultimately survived that battle and went on to win the Senate seat. For the next six years he'll be as safe and sound in his job as he was during Vietnam.

The only real variables during an election season are the candidates themselves. Even they are often interchangeable with politicians of times past, but they bring their own nuance and scandal to keep things interesting. Much of what they say could have come from any other number of campaigns, really, for they're all using the same political playbook. Some are simply better at playing the game.

They all seem to share the same template for speeches. None of us would be surprised if we were to discover that they all shared a pirated copy of Microsoft Speech Generator Deluxe. We can expect to be told what we want to hear. We can expect the usual buzzwords and references to the greatness of the country and we know every speech ends with a "God bless." And we can always expect to be asked for support. Not just rah-rah support, not just throw-a-bumper-sticker-on-the-Chevy support, but *here's my wallet* support. It seems a little galling that someone could jog down the stairs of a private plane, approach a crowd and ask them for money, but this is politics and things seldom make sense.

THE PRIMARY ELECTION

Every four years, our nation's two major (and, if we're honest, only) political parties treat us to the wondrous spectacle of the primary election. During this important time, where the Democratic and Republican candidates for president will be selected, politicians of all stripes descend upon and pretend to care about Iowa, New Hampshire, Maine, Wyoming and others and treat them like a drunken fat girl at a frat party. She gets a little attention, they get what they want and then everyone moves on.

It is during this time that you'll find our country's power elite mingling awkwardly with locals, wandering around uncomfortably in overalls, standing in bowling alleys for the first time in their lives, shouldering firearms awkwardly and generally setting up whatever photo op is necessary to convey that they're just like us. *Look, I sip cheap beer too!*

Are they just like us? Well, they get free health care and are seldom punished for cheating on their taxes. So we're 0 for 2.

I'd like to think most of us are not fooled by this charade one bit and that we know these men and women wouldn't be caught dead doing any of this nonsense were it not for the army of photographers standing by to document their windsurfing (I am young and athletic!), their brush clearing (I'm no privileged son, I'm country!), their baby holding (I am a devoted mom!) and their tearing up (I am losing the primary to a black guy with a Muslim name!).

The pandering to us common folk is uncomfortable to experience. You feel bad for these people, kind of, their immovable hair, forced smiles, freshly pressed and never-before-worn L.L. Bean plaid shirt. These awkward beings are trailed by entourages of BlackBerry-wielding minions, all of them somewhat stunned by having been sucked out of their natural environment and transported to rural cow pastures, dingy country bars, lightbulb factories and decrepit housing projects. In other words, America. They find themselves in a world without air-conditioning. A world where people don't have college degrees. Or all their teeth. Or brokerage accounts. There's faux wood paneling, and people who don't know what *faux* means. Fluorescent lighting. Rifle racks, and dung.

It all has to be perfectly terrible for them as they pretend to understand the plight of the dairy farmer talking to them, pretend to relate to the mom who has five kids and no job, pretend to be the equals of people who say "ain't got no" and "don't have none." It's all so very awkward, so very uncomfortable. But then you have the primary debates.

The primary debate puts an aspiring presidential candidate in the highly uncomfortable position of having to be far more calculated and restrained than anyone is used to being. After all, when you're taking on the other party there are no holds barred. The safety's off and you're free to open fire. But the primary is just you and your own tribesmen and women. Punch too hard, sling too much mud and you might find yourself drummed out of committees and ducking into bathrooms to avoid passing colleagues in the hall. You run the risk of empowering the other party by giving them ammunition for the future. And you imperil your own future by potentially alienating your own constituents. Should you fail to secure the nomination yourself, your actions and words might come back to haunt you later as you find yourself unceremoniously booted off of the vice presidential short list.

Alas, if you go too easy on your opponents you might very well empower them or come across as a milquetoast and lose the nomination altogether, and by having a poor showing at the polls find yourself ruled out as a potential VP pick. It's a delicate balancing act—like being a gay A-list actor with a wife and kids.

But it's even more complicated! Should you be savvy enough to actually clinch the nomination you might very well find that the best, most strategic choice for VP is someone you'd previously trashed as an incompetent boob:

"Larry is not the mechanic you want. He cuts corners. He has questionable knowledge of how the carburetor works. The last car he worked on fell apart on the highway. And he lied about graduating from the Apex School of Technology."

Have fun explaining why you then want to bring Larry on as a partner.

CAMPAIGN ADS

By now, in this cynical, know-it-all world we live in, there should not be a single one of us—not one—who listens to or watches a political advertisement and believes a single thing said in it. By all means, enjoy them for the entertaining spectacle they provide. Enjoy them for the blatant dishonesty, the grainy shots of the evil opponent, the out-of-context newspaper clippings, the molehills turned into mountains, the hum of the threatening soundtrack. It's all truly enjoyable and wonderful. But do not for a single moment allow a single idea from such a production to establish any kind of foothold in your brain. Take it in, savor it and allow it all to pass through you totally undigested, like a kernel of corn.

Every election season the media all find themselves asking the same question: *Are campaign ads more negative than the last time? Are they going too far?* The answer is always, obviously, *Yes*. Nevertheless they assemble panels of political commentators, campaign advisors, various "experts" and the people who actually produce this schlock, who then all sit around and opine. They discuss the reasons they think the ads went negative. They discuss what they could do to focus on the positive. They shake their heads as they discuss and debunk the worst of the lot—the most egregious offenders who stretched the truth the most, fabricated the most, punched below the belt the most. Then everyone goes home and all is forgotten.

But we should certainly let them keep making the things—it's great money for production crews, actors, broadcast outlets and makers of eerie music. I mean, it's usually great money—when the candidates actually pay their bills. Many candidates have a problem doing that, especially when they lose. I once worked on a commercial for a humorless weasel of a Massachusetts politician who lived with his mom. He lost. He never paid us. Naturally, he had been running for *treasurer*.

Despite the deadbeats, it's still a great industry. It's shovel ready! So let people work tirelessly on campaign ads. It's just terribly important that you the consumer realize that nothing, *nothing* you're hearing and seeing is true. It's a thirty-second work of fiction—or a sixty-second work of fiction if the candidate is a billionaire. The only part you can actually believe is the one at the end, where the candidate says he or she approves the message. It's true. They do.

We know politics is heavy on mistruth, and we know advertising is heavy on mistruth, so we should not be the slightest bit surprised at the end result of combining the purveyors of lies with the disseminators of lies. If you ever walk away from a political ad believing that Candidate X kicks puppies or Candidate Y will cut taxes, the ad has done its job but you have not done yours.

POLLSTERS

One of the biggest lies that a politician can tell you is that they don't care what the polls say. They do. Numerous organizations—Pew, Rasmussen, Gallup, Harris, Zogby to name a small handful—run about during any election cycle, asking people for whom they'll be casting their vote. I don't know anyone who cares to answer these, but a lot of people apparently do. To all those answers they collect they then apply their varied, secret methodologies to ultimately arrive at a number that is then broadcast to all of us, to let us know just how Candidate X is faring. If the results favor Mr. X then his supporters cheer them, share them with anyone who'll listen and do a quick happy dance until the next numbers come in. If the results show Candidate X is instead falling behind, then his supporters beg to differ, challenge the methodology, counter with their own numbers or simply assail the source. "Polls are an inexact science," they say, or, "That particular pollster is biased against my candidate."

So, the news is always good or it's wrong. It's a win-win, really.

Polls can be wrong. Harry Truman was predicted to lose the 1948 election to Thomas Dewey in a landslide and didn't. Which begets the question: Can polls influence the vote? If a poll states that your candidate of choice is 30 points behind, would you bother to make your way through a blizzard to vote? Likewise, if a poll says your candidate enjoys a comfortable lead, would you bother to make your way through a blizzard to vote?

My recommendation is that you vote regardless of what the polls might say—if you are inclined to actually vote. Or even better, do your own polling. During the 2004 presidential election I asked my accountant, a lifelong Democrat, what he thought of John Kerry. Not only was my lifelong Democrat accountant not voting for Kerry, he absolutely *loathed* him. I had no clever methodology, and I'd only surveyed one person, but I took that to mean Kerry was in trouble. No idea what the other pollsters said, but my analysis turned out to be correct.

It didn't take much to determine the outcome of the 2008 election either. When half of New York City and their kids were walking around in Obama shirts, it was clear that he had a strong lead. I took the one girl I saw in an inexplicable "Democrats for McCain" shirt to be an anomaly—certainly not any indication of a wider underground political movement that threatened Obama. Since New York City, like Los Angeles, is absurdly unbalanced, I knew I shouldn't arrive at any conclusion until sampling from elsewhere. When two Republican friends told me they were unenthused about

McCain and frightened of Palin, I came to the conclusion (again, with no methodology or intelligent analysis) that his campaign was doomed. I'm thinking about starting a polling company.

DEBATES

Debates, especially the presidential ones, present us with a dilemma. On one hand they're pretty much a complete waste of our time because it's damn well certain that we're not going to learn anything new. We can expect that the candidates have a certain number of things they'd like to drill into our brains by the end of the debate, and we know they will repeatedly say those things whether or not they have anything to do with what is actually being discussed in the course of it.

"Speaking of farm subsidies, I am completely in favor of a ballistic missile shield."

Moderators have a better chance of lassoing a gerbil than getting a politician to actually answer the question that was asked. They try and try, to no avail, to justify their existence by redirecting the conversation to get the yes-or-no answer everyone is waiting for. The politician deftly evades their efforts, magically managing to segue between two completely unrelated topics, leaving all of us scratching our heads. We turn to our significant others and as dazed as we were at the end of *Inception* ask them, "Wait, the question about Medicare?"

In any other environment than a debate our country's politicians would be considered completely, irrevocably insane:

"How are you today, Mark?"

"Lemons."

"I'm sorry, what?"

"Lemons. They're citrus. They grow on trees."

"Mark, I asked you how you were today."

"Lemons are yellow."

On the other hand, debates can on rare occasions offer up those little gems that become historical moments. Miss those and you'll be out of the loop at the water cooler the next day. Usually these immortal quips come in the form of inspired, unscripted one-liners fired off at just the right time. When they're good, they're *real* good and the audience cheers. This forces the moderator to break from trying to get his or her damn question answered and instead ask the audience to shut up.

Lloyd Bentsen went to his grave knowing that even though he didn't get to be vice president, he'd offered up one of the biggest smackdowns in vice-presidential debate history. His "You're no Jack Kennedy" moment made Dan Quayle's eyes water and has been emulated numerous times ever since. It was only a temporary setback and Quayle coasted to victory on Bush the Elder's coattails—where he went on to entertain the world with his shit-eating grin and apparent lack of knowledge of anything of substance.

Likewise, Ronald Reagan did what John McCain could not, and turned the negative of his age into a positive. Asked if he was too old to be president, Reagan famously stated, "I am not going to exploit, for political purposes, my opponent's youth and inexperience." Even his Democratic opponent, Walter Mondale, laughed, and later admitted he believed it to be a harbinger of doom for his campaign.

Ultimately, debates should be taken for what they are: someone repeatedly muttering the same phrase as they meander through a minefield.

GET OUT
THE UNINFORMED ELECTORATE

Every year in the run-up to an election we've come to expect the endless parade of celebrities of all stripes—actors, musicians, talk show hosts, reality show "stars" and whoever else is available—urging us to get out the vote, rock the vote or in the case of Sean P. Puff Daddy Puffy Diddy Combs, the absurdly hyperbolic "Vote or Die." It's our right and responsibility, they tell us; it's what makes democracy work. It's important to vote. Because we can vote. And we all should vote. So, make sure to vote. No matter what, just get out there and vote.

Really?

The idea that we should encourage a mass stampede to the polls simply because we're fortunate enough to have the right to vote seems to be tremendously flawed. Should we be urging people with driver's licenses to hit the road, just for the sake of it? Drive because you're old enough to?

You have a license. You can drive. On November second I hope you will get in your car and start driving. It doesn't matter where you go. Just go there.

Study after study reveals an increasingly uninformed electorate—large numbers of eligible voters who are profoundly ignorant of the issues and the candidates they would be voting on. Many of them don't bother to vote. *Good.* Why would we want them to? Why are we ushering them out of the house and directing them to go vote? A lot of them couldn't even tell you who their congressional representatives are. They think Iraq attacked us on 9/11, or Barack Obama is going to pay their mortgage. Many can't even justify their party affiliation—offering halfhearted explanations for their lifelong tenure as a D or R. One woman told the *Las Vegas Sun* she chose Brian Sandoval for Nevada governor because "he's hot," while another let her husband pick whom she should vote for. Are these people we should be corralling toward the polls on election day? Does it serve a democracy to beg someone to get off their ass, enter a booth and vote for a candidate based on a poster he passed on the street, or something his uncle said? What about the cleverly worded ballot initiatives that most people see for the first time when they're standing in the booth?

The fact that *The Man Show* could have a recurring (and highly successful) gag where they set up a booth and got people to sign a petition to "end women's suffrage" should be indication enough that instead of shepherding the masses to polling stations, we should be directing them toward remedial education centers.

THE CONCESSION

The concession speech seems to be the one moment in a candidate's career when he or she is exhibiting some semblance of honesty. They may have been putting on a happy face during the campaign, and even during the run-up to what was sure to be a defeat, but the concession carries with it the inescapable finality. The admission of defeat. The realization that huge sums of money have been essentially wasted in getting to this awkward point where you must now wish luck on the opponent you demonized and who demonized you for so long. *Awkward* doesn't begin to describe it.

When the fight is over and the losing candidate has been humbled, his human qualities can't help but ooze out. A little, anyway. Inevitably, as with the bully who provoked you to the point of throwing a punch and breaking his nose, you feel a sense of regret.

On occasion we're even moved to feel sorry for them. A little, anyway. In some ways, even though we may have had no intention of voting for John McCain, we could be made to feel bad for him during his concession. For starters, it was clearly his last concession as a presidential candidate. You can't help but feel a little sorry about that, knowing that in the back of the man's head was a little, angry voice spitting and cursing and letting him know he'd never reach the nation's highest office.

Concessions are an awkward way to end months, even years of mudslinging. In fact, it is one of the inherently fascinating qualities of politicians that they are able, the moment a race has been decided, to brush off all the insults, lies, chicanery and duplicity to which they'd been subjected for so long, and extend an olive branch and express a desire to work together for the future. I have no idea how they do it, since most of us would probably unleash a string of swears before storming offstage and hopping a taxi.

In fact, that would seem to be the most human response—so perhaps the concession speech isn't human at all.

12

I've Prepared a Few Words
Free speech(es)

THE CANDIDATE

Ladies and gentlemen,

Washington is broken. And by that I mean I'm not part of it.

I was born into fabulous wealth, the kind that most of you cannot even begin to imagine. Presumably I could burn stacks of hundred-dollar bills in my mansion's fireplaces and not notice any significant deterioration of my wealth. My wine cellar could easily put your kids through college.

We have nothing in common. That is beyond certain. It pains me to have had to touch your hands earlier. And you have ugly babies. Nevertheless, I don't suffer the slightest bit of discomfort in standing before you, in all your lower- and middle-classness, to ask you to support my run for office. I would like not only your votes, but your financial assistance as well. And I ask that you offer these things enthusiastically.

I would like to hear some thunderous applause now, so allow me to say that I love this country. This is the greatest country in the world. There is no other country that is better. And you—you before me all represent the real America, not those people in the other part of America who aren't here right now.

Now, let me bring in the military thing. I know the importance of serving your country while not actually being in harm's way when doing so. For that reason, I joined the Reserve. There, with the assistance of my family's powerful connections, I was able to add a military stint to my résumé, while at the same time greatly reducing the risk that I might possibly get sent off somewhere to be injured or killed, thus derailing my preordained career.

I know. I know. Life is not fair.

I'd be remiss not to mention that absent the requirement of merit, I was able to attend a prestigious university. It too looks very good on my résumé, and as you can imagine was on the list of things I had to do before I found myself standing here, before you, asking for your help. Believe me, if there was a way to get around having to do this I would, but it's an unfortunate necessity if you want to achieve political office in the greatest country on earth!

I'd like to hear some more cheering at this point, so let's salute the heroes of our military!

I also very much understand the importance of God to you. So allow me to mention how important my faith is to me and my family, and to share with you an anecdote from my church. Having done that, I hope that you'll realize I'm not an atheist, because I am well aware that those types never get elected. Freedom!

It is perhaps ironic that with your assistance I will find myself in a position to protect my enormous wealth and acquire even more. However, I realize I cannot achieve my goals without your help. To accomplish this I am willing to say whatever it takes to get you to vote for me. I am hoping that you will take what I say at face value, disregard the glaring untruths and believe wholeheartedly in my carefully crafted message.

My message is not necessarily one of belief or principle. It comes not from the heart but from political expediency. I may not believe in the importance or true value of everything I am saying, but my highly paid campaign strategists have told me that you do.

Once in office I will begin to govern based on the needs of my lobbyists. Everything I do will be a calculated maneuver to ensure the happiness of those most important to me: my biggest contributors. If my seat seems to be in peril I will shamelessly pander to you the voter and do what is necessary to retain control. To that end I will work tirelessly for legislation that will reward you in the short term without regard to any potential long-term consequences. For by the time the scale and enormity of my malfeasance and lack of foresight come to light, I will likely no longer be in office, and your anger and disenchantment will be moot.

Please keep cheering and repeating my name for a moment.

Now, this seems like a good time to invoke the children thing. Because many of us have children and we want the world to be a better place for children. For that reason, I'd like to equate your voting for me with you protecting children. Your children. Our children. I will pause for applause now because we should always applaud when talking about our children.

I would like to end by suggesting that I will change things. Despite all the overwhelming evidence to the contrary, I need you to believe that I will be different than the last guy. I need you to forget recent history. I know you want a better tomorrow. And I know that by promising you a better tomorrow, you will be more motivated to vote for me.

This is your chance to think you're going to make a difference. I beg you: Stop thinking and start voting.

Thank you, and God bless America!

THE CONCESSION

I spent a lot of money on this campaign. A lot. Most people can't believe that any one person has that much money. But I did. And I burned through a whole bunch of it. Don't worry, I'm still staggeringly wealthy. My only regret is that I did not spend enough to win this election.

I hate my opponent because he trounced me, but I'm not going to say that because it's politics and I'll need to keep all my options open. I am going to say that he ran a good campaign, but we all know it's a lie. He went negative right out of the gate and beat me to it. I fired back but it was a little too late. And he had even more money than I did. I probably should have gone even more negative, but I'm not sure that was even possible. I all but said he was the biggest piece of shit in the universe, and now here I am talking about him like he's a decent human being.

A lot of people who were hoping to land cushy gigs spent a lot of time and energy working on my campaign. I'd like to thank them. They are very disappointed. So, I am going to try to make them feel better by suggesting that even though we lost, we were able to "make a difference." I'm going to absurdly suggest that my opponent listen to the concerns of the people who voted for me. I'll say something about partisanship and suggest that my opponent reach across the aisle and work with my party. Of course we all know that's an absurd fantasy.

Anyway, I need to start strategizing about my next attempt to get into office. I'm also going to look into moving money from my campaign account into my personal account.

Thank you, and God bless America!

PART THE FOURTH

Knee Deep and Shovel Ready

Wherein, finding ourselves standing in "It,"
we explore ways to get out of "It"

13

THE SEVEN HABITS OF HIGHLY PARTISAN PEOPLE

The partisan people you meet in heaven

Regardless of what side of the political spectrum they've chosen to call home, the partisans among us all share similar habits. These habits help reinforce their partisan-ness, fanning the flames and ultimately leading to those regrettable exchanges we see all over the Twitternet, InterSphere, CyberWeb, FacebookTube and anywhere it's easy for a spirited and amazingly polarized individual to offer his or her two cents.

If we are in danger of being polarized ourselves, or if we are willing to admit that we feel that we may indeed be polarized and willing to get "on the wagon," so to speak, recognizing those habits is important. In doing so, we might better understand the behaviors and tendencies that lead people to say and do things that make no sense, have little foundation in truth or are just plain scary, I give you the Seven Habits of Highly Partisan People:

1. Reliance on Biased News Sources

For the same reason that a devout Baptist doesn't attend a Greek Orthodox mass, partisans are keen to stay within the realm of What I Know to Be True. They like that place! It's comfy-cozy, there are no unpleasant thoughts to contend with and everything is familiar. To stay in that realm all they need to do is carefully narrow down their informational sources to the select ones that provide them with a steady flow of the information they seek and are already inclined to believe. In this day and age there are ridiculous amounts of mostly free sources of information and opinion available to us via television, radio, print and the Internet. Of course, despite the sheer abundance of choices, the partisan is careful to select only those that suit his or her inclination, the ones that provide the comfort of agreement, the ones that keep them within that realm of What I Know to Be True.

For that reason, the partisan wouldn't dream of opening up *Mother Jones* if *National Review* is on the table. Likewise, a regular visitor to dailykos.com would not dare set foot in a horrible place like weeklystandard.com lest he suffer the taint of having shared pixels in cyberspace with people who think affirmative action has run its course. If you're inclined to think that jet plane vapor trails are the government secretly poisoning the air, then you stay in the realm of conspiracy theorist websites and ignore the abundance of sites that point out the obvious.

In the run-up to the first vote on the Health Care Reform Bill an intelligent and politically minded friend of mine made an observation about it in a comment on Facebook. For reasons I still don't understand, I broke from my normal policy of not engaging in political commentary on Facebook and offered up my opinion that the bill probably wasn't a good idea. I don't remember why. Maybe it was because a lot of people didn't want it, or it was going to be phenomenally expensive. Can't recall. Regardless, my short, simple remark prompted an immediate, angry response from someone else in Facebookville—a lady friend of his—who in effect said:

1. I was clearly a stupid person who let Fox News think for me;
2. She was sick of "those kinds of people"; and
3. If I needed to get a clue about the proposed bill I should read up on it—at whitehouse.gov.

I had a few problems with this whole exchange (to which I never responded—never do in those instances) because:

1. I hadn't been addressing her in the first place;
2. She didn't know me from Adam but was happy to assume I was stupid and got all my opinions from Fox News, which I don't watch; and
3. Amid her obnoxious display of smug superiority she directed me to whitehouse.gov, which she clearly considered an objective news source regarding this issue.

If there's a Nobel Prize for partisan snobbery, I nominate her.

Angry Lady is no exception, of course. Every day thousands of individuals get their news solely from *The Daily Show with Jon Stewart* or *Glenn Beck* or Media Matters for America or *The Rachel Maddow Show* or this or that or the other thing. They swallow little oysters of information without sniffing first. Then they forward, re-tweet, embed, cut and paste, or whatever is required to get the news out so that other like-minded individuals can believe and repeat it as well. Hold a microphone in any partisan's face and you'll hear the same points regurgitated over and over again. But ask them to go above and beyond the sound bite they overheard last week and you're liable to stump them. "Eh, uh, well, you know, it just is."

And why should you or would you entertain poisonous ideas from somewhere outside your comfort sphere, your realm of What I Know to Be True? Because sometimes those ideas are *insightful*. Just like when we travel to foreign countries and experience foreign cultures and foods and behavior we learn things, and learning things is never bad.

Case in point: During the TSA security debacle of Holiday Season 2010, when our country's latex-fingered heroes were fondling our private parts to protect us from militant Islam, there was universal, across-the-spectrum outrage against what was largely seen as unacceptably intrusive, ineffective, logic-defying security theater.

If you were to visit the websites of the right, you would have seen the usual complaints about out-of-control government, Islam sucking and terrorists winning, along with more thoughtful statements like "Just be glad that TSA employees were not unionized!" A right-partisan might be very content to stay in that realm. But, were he to wander over to some websites of the left, he would have been exposed to other trains of thought as well, such as "If the TSA was unionized, the workers might be in a position to say no to the pat-down procedures!"

Note: I'm not making an argument for unionizing or not unionizing the TSA. I am making an argument that they are both valid points that would never have entered either partisan's mind had he chosen to remain in his normal realm.

2. Acceptance of Nonsense as Fact

As we headed into the 2010 midterms, most Republicans (and a good helping of Democrats) were hopping mad at Barack Obama for raising taxes. After all, in times of economic turmoil every last penny counts. For this guy to heap more taxes on the suffering people in the middle of an economic crisis? It's unthinkable. Enraging. Insidious.

Oh, and untrue.

There are plenty of reasons to have a grievance with the Obama administration, but the president's supposed immediate implementation of higher taxes was not one of them. Cuts aimed at helping middle-class families served 95 percent of the working population. Of course "helped" is relative, but the cuts, breaks for education and the other incentives didn't exactly make things worse. Should you put him past raising taxes in the future? No, of course not! He's a politician!

But the rage over tax hikes is not based in reality.

Nevertheless, a Bloomberg poll revealed that 52 percent of likely voters believed Obama hiked middle-class taxes in the first two years of his administration. More than half the likely voters were under the impression that the president hiked taxes. How does that happen? How do people believe something that simply is not true?

Because it fits the narrative they want it to fit. Validation blinders, activate!

Partisans like to have their beliefs validated—that's why they'll take anything that's tossed their way even if the source is unreliable. They'll form opinions based on emails someone forwarded them because they wanted to have those opinions. Smart people I know were convinced Obama got the Pledge of Allegiance wrong and they had the photographic proof. Furious, they distributed the photo around their corner of the e-universe. "Look! This guy doesn't even know how to do the Pledge!" Sure enough, there was the photo of the president of the United States with the wrong hand over his chest. But did anyone notice that his lapel pin was on the other side? Or his buttons? No, they didn't have time to, because they were busy forwarding their outrageous (and altered) photo to everyone in their address book. Once again, the desire to see the president as they want him to be (in this case, un-American) overwhelms the partisan type, and causes him or her to lose all ability to critically evaluate before disseminating junk.

The export of nonsense isn't limited to obscure websites or mass emails either. It comes to us regularly via the media. One of the more egregious examples of this came from an interview between MSNBC host Rachel Maddow and Kentucky candidate for U.S. Senate Rand Paul. In a previous interview, Maddow had treated Paul with kid gloves—because he wasn't a threat. *Look, a kooky guy with kooky ideas!* As the race progressed and the odds of that Senate seat actually going to a Republican increased, the gloves came off. In a subsequent interview Maddow asked Paul if he agreed with the Civil Rights Act. Anyone familiar with the libertarian viewpoint understood his clumsy answer. What Paul was trying to say is that while he supported the ends, he didn't support the government dictating what a private enterprise had to do—a very libertarian position. Maddow and many on the left—some cluelessly but most disingenuously—took his response to mean "I do not support civil rights." He was immediately labeled as a racist and it was damage control from that point onward.

Had she asked Paul if he believed no-smoking laws should be mandatory he would likely have said it should be "up to the business." Not an endorsement of smoking, but a libertarian position. Maddow and friends might have taken that to mean Paul advocates getting lung cancer.

3. Rejection of Alternate Viewpoints

My friend's wife was very, very pro-health-care reform. She made her stance abundantly clear on Facebook in the days leading up to the first failed attempt to pass it.

Anyone within shouting range of her status update knew how she felt about it and her contention that we should support it, and that it would be good for us and good for America. Like a lot of people, I disagreed, but there was no point in commenting—I didn't know her enough to engage in a debate and I'd have nothing to gain from it if I did. Just prior to the vote she topped off her steady barrage of highly political updates with this ultimatum: "If you don't support affordable health care, maybe you shouldn't be my friend."

I would think everyone supports the idea of affordable health care—they just can't agree on how to go about actually achieving it in a sensible, cost-effective way, or if the government should be involved in the process at all. Nevertheless, her point was clear: If you don't agree with *my view*, go away. Taking her up on her offer was easy—a few clicks later her thoughts no longer occupied my corner of cyberspace. Mind you, the final straw wasn't her incessant, nagging support for legislation that she (like the people crafting it) likely knew very little about. Rather, it was her obnoxious display of intolerance in the suggestion that merely to disagree with her was a capital offense. Partisan.

Is disagreement really that bad? Is someone holding a different viewpoint intolerable? Frankly, I would think it highly unpleasant to be surrounded by only like-minded individuals. What could be more boring than a roomful of people in total agreement on everything? Have we not been told, time and again, year after year, mindlessly and endlessly to *celebrate diversity*? Does that not include the diversity of opinion? Well, we know where my former "friend" stands but what about you? Do you banish nonbelievers from your kingdom . . . or do you, one hopes, find joy in celebrating the diversity of opinion?

Jamming one's fingers in one's ears like this is hardly respectable, yet we see variations of it quite frequently. When Whoopi Goldberg and Joy Behar storm away after Bill O'Reilly's awkwardly worded "Muslims killed us on 9/11," the only point they are making is "I am unwilling to entertain a viewpoint that is different than mine." And if you're unwilling to tolerate dissent, if talking something out is absolutely not an option, where do you go from there? The Bush administration rebuffed more than one attempt from Iran to establish a dialogue and we know how well that worked out: An absolute nutter like Mahmoud Ahmadinejad came to power and started mocking us as he set about building a bomb.

This rejection of alternate viewpoints also manifests itself in the insistence that the bearer of unwanted news is either just plain wrong or unforgivably biased. We're not talking about disreputable websites or self-proclaimed experts either, but rather legitimate, long-standing news sources. That the *New York Times* leans left is no longer a secret—if it ever was a secret to begin with—but to many individuals it's no less a propaganda outlet than *Pravda*. That's unfortunate.

4. Chronic Memory Loss

Prior to the 2004 Republican National Convention in New York City, a mass of humanity, in numbers I'd never before seen, marched through the streets of Manhattan on their way toward Madison Square Garden. Because they chose to march past my window, I had front-row seats to this awesome spectacle. On the one hand, it was a fantastic display of our First Amendment rights, and of the fact that in this country you can make your grievances known without being bludgeoned, jailed, tortured or executed. The kind of display of displeasure toward the government and its officials that many, many people the world over are unable to put on—be they in Burma, Iran, Russia, Zimbabwe or Syria—let's face it, you can't get away with that crap in a lot of the world. That's what makes us luckier than a lot of the world.

But the freedom to say what you want to say comes at a price: You have to suffer the idiocy of those who would compare leaders with whom they disagree to Hitler.

I was no fan of George W. Bush and his hapless band of corporatists and bumblers, but I'm also no fan of equating people you don't like with Hitler. There were the BUSH = HITLER placards, Bush's face superimposed over a saluting Hitler's body, Bush with Hitler's trademark toothbrush mustache and of course swastikas, swastikas, swastikas: Bush wearing one, Bush spelled with one, the U.S. flag with swastikas instead of stars. It was upsetting, stupendously dumb and very hard to explain to my mother-in-law, who was visiting from Poland.

Naturally, Bush supporters complained loudly. People like me—those who felt the Nazi comparisons cheapened the atrocities committed by the Nazis—complained as well. There was no short-age of people on the left who, faced with these criticisms, the outrage and indignation, pretty much shrugged their shoulders. Likewise the images of Bush in a rifle's crosshairs, or the burning effigies, the Bush dangling from a noose or the straight-to-the-point "Kill Bush" signs, received the same collective "Meh" whenever it was brought up.

Oh, and how could we forget the 2006 film *Death of a President*? The fake documentary was a hypothetical look back at the aftermath of the unsolved assassination of President George W. Bush. The right was absolutely livid, the left absolutely amused.

Fast-forward to the protests of 2010 and lo and behold *he's baaaack*! "He" being Hitler of course. But now the shoe was on the other foot. The powerless placard holders of 2004 were now the sup-porters of the ones in power. And the angry crowds holding signs were different. This time Barack Obama was Hitler. Nancy Pelosi was Hitler! Harry Reid was Hitler!

Oh, touché!

Did the Obama crowd have a lightbulb moment and remember their own "Bushitler" signs and stickers and swastikas of only a few years ago? No! No they did not. They were nothing short of out-raged. "How dare you compare *my guy* to Hitler!"

They declared such comparisons uncalled for and unacceptable, and said the same about the inevitable threatening placards and any-thing that could be perceived as a threat. They wanted retractions and apologies.

What short memories partisans have.

5. Acute Hypocrisy

There exists in the partisan sphere of politics a system of shifting standards as applied to your position on the political spectrum. The bar is set much higher for any fool on the other end, while on the partisan's end the bar is as low as the situation requires. Whether that bar determines what is considered criminal, impeachable, despicable or immoral, left and right never seem to achieve parity. The condemnable, outrageous offenses of your guy are merely unimportant transgressions when it turns out to be mine.

The partisans on the left can point their fingers at Governor Mark Sanford, Senator Larry Craig, Senator John Ensign and plenty other fools, and laugh at their malfeasance and failure and scandal and shame. At the same time they restrain judgment of their own behaviorally challenged ranks, shrugging off or excusing away the crotch-driven deeds of former governor (and TV star) Eliot Spitzer, former governor (and TV star) Jim McGreevey, or the reigning king of genitally motivated malfeasance, former president (and current superstar) Bill Clinton. Unfortunately for John Edwards, he's fair game for anyone—but only because he'd gone far enough to have made his perfectly sculpted hair and poorly functioning brain politically unviable.

And therein the partisan hypocrisy lies: "As long as it suits my party and my politics, it's okay." They don't come out and say that, of course, and they may not even realize that's what they feel, but that *is* how they feel. When called out on such bias, partisans will claim that their particularly enhanced umbrage was due to the politician's own hypocrisy—the Family Values Crusader caught with his pants down. And that's fair enough, but it's not honest enough, for if they truly sought the moral high ground and delighted in seeing a blatant hypocrite suffer for his sins then there would be no greater recent candidate than Eliot Spitzer, who aggressively prosecuted prostitution while also making use of its services. Alas, it's seldom the case that someone of a polarized nature can actually see that.

Spitzer suffered the indignity of leaving his elected office, but was soon inexplicably rewarded with an unwatchable TV show.

Armed with only one viewpoint, having no desire to consider any others and equipped with the resulting shortsightedness that it produces, the partisan sort can, without reservation, storm into a town hall and make demands that are inherently, absurdly hypocritical.

It would be funny if it wasn't so frustrating that *Rolling Stone* reporter Matt Taibbi could interview two Tea Party members at a rally, self-described as "anti-spending and anti-government" and come to learn one is a tax assessor and the other is sitting on her Medicare-provided mobility scooter. Responding to Taibbi's challenge that a lifetime government worker and a Medicare recipient's anti-welfare/government position made no sense, the husband responds, in essence, that he and his wife don't really count because he doesn't make very much.

And yet day in, day out we find ourselves tripping over our jaws as we watch recipients of handouts opposing handouts, SUV owners shaking their fists at oil companies and actors taking a break in between their $20 million gigs to embrace a murderous dictator and rail against capitalism.

6. Defense of the Indefensible

It serves as testimony to the blinding nature of partisanship that individuals can so easily engage in the knee-jerk defense of their preferred politicians even when that person's conduct is unquestionably abysmal and actually at odds with the defender's personal mores and values. Honest and devoted spouses will excuse a philandering politico's atrocious transgressions; a dutiful taxpayer will accept any explanation tendered to explain his official's financial improprieties. There is no transgression, character flaw or weakness that cannot be overcome, merely by diminishing its import or excusing it altogether. For the partisan, being on the same team warrants a level of forgiveness that would not be bestowed upon errant coworkers, friends or even family members.

Herein lies the danger faced by overly forgiving partisans: You may choose to be as blind or softhearted of your candidates as you'd like, but that can very well come back and bite you. The 2010 midterms offered several candidates whose flaws—excused and shrugged off by supporters—in many cases proved too much for the rest to bear. Case in point: Christine O'Donnell, whose résumé was as impressive as dinner at IHOP, whose financial history raised red flags, whose legacy of TV appearances was embarrassing, whose debate performance was poor and whose senatorial demeanor was absent. It was at this point that an individual, being honest with him or herself, should have simply stopped telling us how great she was and admitted the truth: "She's awful, I know, but I just don't like Chris Coons."

No wonder so many politicians wind up with delusions of omnipotence—they can behave like cretins, boors, scoundrels and mountebanks and still find no shortage of eager defenders who'd fall on their swords before admitting their man was anything other than a poor, delicate, innocent victim of misunderstanding, conspiracy or persecution. Power corrupts, but it certainly gets plenty of help from the likes of folks who'll excuse egregious behavior when it suits them.

7. Conduct Unbecoming

Obi Wan Kenobi, describing the city of Mos Eisley, put it thusly: "You will never find a more wretched hive of scum and villainy." The same could certainly be said for the Internet. The distance and anonymity it offers us emboldens, on a grand scale, even the most feeble, weak-kneed and delicate members of our society be they male or female, twelve or forty, muscular or blobular. Free to redefine themselves in this virtual world and more important, not afraid of being punched in the face, they become valiant warrior wordslingers armed with a battery of epithets, swears, insults and threats as well as a bandolier of snazzy clichés to deploy whenever necessary. Add to that a partisan streak, and the Internet becomes a very dangerous place indeed. It's like the worst bar in the worst part of town in the worst city that you can think of. (Personally I think of Detroit; your mileage may vary.)

Fights start at the drop of a hat and get brutal fast. No punches are pulled and opponents are quick to go for the jugular. What can trigger such ungentlemanly mayhem and poisonous invective? Oh, a hint of disagreement, the suggestion you like the wrong official or might be against a particular policy. It doesn't take much, especially when no one has anything to lose and fists can't travel though your modem. Civility is dead, and you'll realize this the moment your eloquently worded response to someone's misunderstanding of the First Amendment gets you called a "pussy-ass bitch." Ironically, in addressing you this way, your verbal assailant is actually exercising the First Amendment rights he didn't understand only a few messages previous.

Yes, the partisan sort is an emotional creature, prone to fits of pique and often quite willing to dispense with pleasantries, eloquence and sophistication in favor of the swiftness and ease of simply calling you "dipshit."

14

PARTISANS ANONYMOUS
A twelve-step recovery program

Unlike Mel Gibson and several high-end country clubs, partisan political intoxication doesn't discriminate. It's an equal-opportunity affliction that, if left untreated, can progress to the point where it has a tremendously damaging effect on your mental health, family, social life and even career. Especially if you tell your boss he voted for a blithering idiot.

If, having read the previous chapter, you believe you exhibit some or all of the characteristics of a partisan person, you will find this chapter helpful in guiding you toward the pathway that winds its way to the staircase of self-awareness that deposits you on the sidewalk to recovery.

Likewise, if you believe you know someone—perhaps a friend, coworker, loved one, loved coworker or working friend—who exhibits symptoms of partisanship, please encourage them to buy several copies of this book so that they might be guided out of the dark forest of cloudy judgment to the meadow of clarity that borders the stream of enlightenment, while at the same time helping to increase book sales.

No matter what, do not despair. You can do it! Recovery can be challenging; it could possibly be the biggest struggle you've faced since trying to install Windows Vista. But it is far from impossible. In due time, you could find yourself standing on the precipice of joy on the mountain of objectivity, with a breathtaking view of the valley of bad metaphors.

Remember, you do not have to give in to partisanship. There is *always* hope. And change.

EARLY DETECTION

Early signs of partisan political intoxication (PPI) include engaging in frequent debate with others, or alone, and the willingness to enter dangerous, uncharted waters despite the risks. Politically intoxicated individuals can undergo a significant change of demeanor, becoming irascible and even violent at times. They may later express remorse at having taken such a strong position or may even not remember what exactly their position was, as a result of having been so energetically engaged. This is called a blackout.

There is no definitive "type" of person who can develop PPI. They can be young or old, left-wing or right-wing, black or white (or the other ones) and rich, poor or middle class—if there is a middle class left by the time this book reaches you. There may or may not be a family history. A lot of sufferers deny being partisan and will have to come to realize it on their own terms. Do not underestimate the

power of the human mind to deny reality! Remember, it took decades before people had any inkling about Liberace.

RECOGNIZING THE SYMPTOMS

Sometimes we may be blind to our affliction. For reasons that could
very well be subconscious, we fail to connect the dots and fully comprehend how low we've actually gone. The first step to recovery is
recognizing the problem—ideally before hitting rock bottom.

In addition to possessing some or all of the qualities mentioned
in the preceding chapter, an individual afflicted with chronic partisanship will exhibit an assortment of related symptoms. Sometimes
the symptoms are very pronounced; other times they're much more
subtle. Knowing what they are and being on the lookout for them
can help you push the button of awareness that calls the elevator of
transformation that will take you to the floor of enlightenment. Or
you can take the stairs, which is healthier but takes a little longer.

If some of these symptoms listed below seem familiar to you,
then it's a good indication that your partisanship (or that of your
loved one/coworker) may have progressed to a dangerous level and is
worthy of taking action.

Remember, partisanship is a progressive disease. And by "progressive" I don't mean Glenn-Beck-running-around-screaming-about-
Woodrow-Wilson progressive, but rather the "developing in stages"
progressive.

The important thing is to recognize the symptoms and take action. Left untreated, partisan political intoxication will eventually
leave you standing all alone in the middle of a pasture shouting at
flowers.

Symptoms of partisan political intoxication:

- LOSS OF FACEBOOK FRIENDS. Individuals may notice a decline in the number of friends he or she has on the time-wasting, privacy-squandering social network. Or they may sense that people have perhaps "hidden" their updates from view after one too many rants about the Food Safety Act, the Koch Brothers or Net Neutrality.

- SHUNNING AND SHUSHING. Individuals may notice at office parties, alumni gatherings and dinners out that they are either consciously being avoided or constantly being asked to "talk about something else for Christ's sake."

- POOR WORK PERFORMANCE. Individuals may find their productivity suffers because, instead of doing their job, they find themselves increasingly engaged in long-winded debates about tax reform, the Tenth Amendment and gun control with strangers on buzzing hive websites like Democracy Underground or Free Republic.

- TOPIC ABUSE. The afflicted individual has a tendency to steer even the most casual conversation about the weather in to an angry diatribe about public sector employee pensions. Even the most mundane event—such as a flight cancellation, price hike or flu shot promotion—is perceived as being political in nature, in the same way that Al Sharpton sees traffic, heavy winds or getting a parking ticket as evidence of racism.

- HUMORLESSNESS. The individual has diminished humor capacity, and difficulty laughing at anything perceived as an attack on his or her party or political stance. For example, a Republican partisan may not find humor in the fact that John Boehner is orange.

- IMPAIRED CONTROL. The individual is completely unable to refrain from opinioneering even when in an environment that would make doing so awkward, uncalled for or totally inappropriate. For example, launching into a polemic about the government being in the pocket of the health insurance companies as his infant child is exiting the womb.
- DECREASED TOLERANCE. The individual is unable to stomach even the slightest counteropinion without becoming enraged or irritated. The announcement that one might vote for an incumbent or that the postal service isn't completely terrible can result in a brutal verbal altercation or unwarranted ad hominem attacks.
- WITHDRAWAL. Individuals find themselves isolated from friends and family because they are repeatedly excusing themselves so that they may access Twitter, Facebook, Drudge Report, Daily Kos and numerous unsavory websites in an effort to feed their constant desire for information and expression.

THE STEPS TO RECOVERY

If you've recognized any of those symptoms of partisanship in yourself and you want to take action, then you are already halfway to the airport in the taxi of understanding, on your way to take a budget airline flight to the paradise of sanity and calm thoughts—as soon as TSA gets done radiating you or massaging your private parts. For freedom.

Below are twelve steps. If you lived by them every single day, well, that would be weird. But if you keep them tucked in the back of your mind—wherever you keep those important memories like where your keys are, or the combination to your luggage lock—then you will be doing better than the millions of people who every day are forced to suffer from their partisan addiction.

THE TWELVE STEPS OF PARTISAN RECOVERY

1. Admit that you are powerless over partisanship.

Step back and take a deep breath. As long as politics isn't seizing your house and sending you and your family to a forced labor camp in Alaska, you're doing okay. Yes, politics can be a huge pain in the bum, and yes, it can make your life a little miserable, but how miserable? If it's revolution miserable, then by all means, go foment one. Otherwise, refrain from letting politics become a corrosive substance that finds its way into every crack and crevice and contaminates everything in your life. It can make you miserable. Don't be the person who is ranting and raving about politics all the time. No one wants to be stuck in a car pool with that guy.

2. Acknowledge that debate can restore you to sanity.

You know what? Even the most simple of human beings (and yes, I was immediately thinking of the Housewives of New Jersey) are complex in their opinions. They can have a wide range of beliefs and positions that can be bizarre, contradictory, insane, stupid and otherwise. And that's fine. Because diversity of opinions is a good thing. And the fact that we live in a country where we can express them openly and not be jailed, harassed or killed is an even better thing. We're all bound to disagree on an abundance of items, but

what makes any democracy strong is the free exchange of ideas. If you were to jot down a list of the least successful countries on the planet, you would eventually come to realize that they are all countries where the freedom of speech and expression have been stifled or eliminated altogether. For a country to achieve any level of greatness requires that ideas, be they good, bad, stupid or brilliant, not be kept hidden in the cupboard.

3. Make a decision not to be a proselytizer.

You are not going to convince someone to change their mind on gun control while sitting at the bar. Nor can you expect someone will come to see things your way during a short bus ride, or at dinner, or during your kid's Little League game. Two reasons: If they have a strong contrary opinion, then you're not going to change them like that. And if they just nod their head as you talk, it means they're not as interested in visa requirements, VAT, relations with Belarus or the Seventeenth Amendment as you are. In those instances, it's much better to talk about something you're likely to agree on, such as <u>Two and a Half Men</u> not being funny or Katy Perry's blatant use of cleavage as a marketing tool.

4. Fearlessly, keep politics where it belongs.

Not every moment is calling out to be interrupted by a position statement or declaration that Congressman So-and-so sucks. If the topic of the conversation was, "Hey, doesn't Congressman So-and-so suck?" by all means, engage and concur or politely disagree. But if the conversation is "Do you think they'll be putting a new Starbucks in that location?" do not take that as an invitation to declare New York mayor Michael Bloomberg to be a calorie-counting, trans-fat and salt-hating nanny-state politician. Even though he is.

5. Admit that volume is not a substitute for knowledge.

You cannot expect larger sound waves to make up for a lack of facts. You can't. Turning it up to 11 is not a legitimate counterargument. Many partisans, by virtue of their knee-jerk tendency to go on the offensive, often find themselves engaged in a debate without a preponderance of facts. This creates a potentially very awkward engagement if the other person actually comes armed with them. The bullhorn approach is an acknowledgment that your argument is not solid, and is a de facto admission of defeat. You do not win an argument by going "Oh yeah! Well I say Social Security is going insolvent! Booyah! Hagoobah! Wooooo!"

If your argument cannot be expressed in your pleasant inside voice, then perhaps it needs to be reevaluated or placed on the back burner for the time being.

6. Consider whether there might be something better you could be doing with your time than indulging your defects of character.

Are you at work? Do your kids miss "old daddy" or "happy mommy"? It might be time to step away from the computer or step down from the soapbox and spend some time with them. Or go scrapbooking. I personally think scrapbooking's a racket, and I don't get it at all, but I'd much rather you be doing that than being all wild and upset about steel tariffs or Medicaid. If we could only harness the energy of the countless hundreds of thousands who are pecking away furiously at keyboards in response to a newspaper article they don't like, or a blog post they disagree with, we'd have enough energy to solve all of our problems and tell all the Saudi princes to take a hike.

7. If you wouldn't say it to their face, don't say it at all.

The Internet is filled with tough guys who curse and threaten and aren't afraid to talk the talk because they know they don't have to walk the walk. Secure in the knowledge that they're two thousand miles away from their targets, who are unwilling and unable to track down someone named h8erkilla77, they're unafraid to unload a host of unpleasantries that would make Eminem blush. Unfortunately, this is about as macho as giving someone the finger and speeding off in a car.

8. Stop with the freaking Hitler crap, already.

The little maniac with the toothbrush mustache and foul temper is responsible for one of the greatest conflicts in world history and a staggering genocide. Millions and millions and millions of people suffered horribly and/or died because of this trembling nutter and all his snazzily dressed friends with their funky logo and well-oiled murder machine. A very bad man indeed. But there is no one on the entire world stage who can or should be compared to him. Stalin and Mao—they're certainly in his league. But they're very dead. Someone declaring that Barack Obama or George W. Bush is Hitler or that whomever they do not like is comparable to Nazis is merely declaring their limited understanding of history and the inability to express ideas beyond a kindergarten level. Until such time as they are annexing countries, sparking global wars, liquidating political opposition and engaging in a massive, mechanized ethnic cleansing effort, your opponent is not Hitler. Even if he sports a stylish mustache like John Bolton.

9. Do some homework.

We all know people who claim to be fluent in a language and then, when pressed for a sentence or two, mumble the incorrectly conjugated phrasebook equivalent of "Where is the bathroom?" before sheepishly explaining that they're not actually fluent, you see, they just happen to know a little bit. So, they're fluent in the same way I'm a professional baseball player because I hit the ball once. In other words, they're full of crap.

A good amount of partisan behavior is based on being full of crap, because of the partisan habit of ignoring facts or logic and focusing solely on shooting the other guy's argument down by any means possible. It becomes not about knowing anything of value that one could incorporate into the discussion, but instead simply about telling the other person that their idea sucks. Arguments like this are unfulfilling, as I imagine a philosophical discussion with a Kardashian might be.

When you do engage in the art of political debate, knowing what you're actually talking about and not being full of crap is empowering. When in the course of a dialogue you are capable of offering up a rebuttal—as opposed to ratcheting up the volume or repeatedly saying whatever you heard on TV the other day—there's a little voice in your head that will go, "Hey! I have information in my head that I am putting to good use!" which you'll likely find rewarding. The information that gets in your head is up to you. There is no shortage of books filled with all sorts of wonderful and interesting information, of course. And websites galore—some of which aren't a total waste of time. And there are policy papers from think tanks. Old fashioned newspapers. Magazines.

My dear friend John, who by virtue of being Irish reads incredible amounts of books, knows simply everything. All I need do is make any statement about anything and he can (and does) immediately respond with "Well, Brian, the flaw in your logic is that in 1827 the Hungarian economist Flurvehr Mergimer once said . . ." And then he rejoices in lecturing me for hours. It's great. For him, mostly.

10. Consider declaring independence.

As a member of a political party you are already inclined to defend it, obey it and take umbrage when you feel it's been slighted. In other words, parties breed the kind of partisanship that many of the Founding Fathers had predicted. Too bad these guys aren't around to offer stock tips.

Freeing oneself from the shackles of party politics and becoming an Independent voter automatically reduces the opportunity and inclination to be partisan. You are free to agree with or find fault with Democrats and Republicans because you aren't one. You can approach your politics on an issue-by-issue basis rather than the take-it-or-leave-it deal the parties offer you. That's a good thing, because it keeps parties on their toes. They can't assume they have your allegiance. They will actually have to earn your vote rather than just come to expect it.

Pollsters and strategists have a terrible time with Independents. They routinely attempt to write them off as partisans in denial and suggest that their power is a myth, yet they also routinely attempt to accommodate them because, at the end of the day the Independent voter is a <u>known unknown</u>. The people doing all the math in the run-up to an election really don't like that.

The parties know they can count on the bulk of their base to be in lockstep on most issues and to vote how they are told, but the Independent? They keep them guessing. In tight races, they keep them guessing and keep them nervous. As we saw in 2008, the Independent swing voter swung largely in the direction of Barack Obama and the Democrats. McCain's attempt to lure women back to his side by selecting Sarah Palin as a running mate failed to work. After all the swingers had swung, he was finished.

Two years later, as the 2010 midterms approached, President Obama and the Democrats clearly understood that the Independent vote was not theirs to claim. The pendulum was headed back in the other direction. Thus began the scramble to coax them back and the eleventh-hour pleas to vote Democrat so that they might "finish the job" they'd been elected to do. <u>Remember election eve 2008? That was electric, wasn't it? Remember that? Hey! Come back!</u>

Unfortunately for them, many of the Independent voters weren't fond of the "let us finish the job" message because they didn't believe the Democrats were doing the job they'd been elected to do. The other message, "Uh, the Republicans are worse," failed to work as well. The swingers swung back and treated the Democrats to the Grand Spanking of 2010.

All of this should be empowering to the Independent because it shows that as much as the two major parties would like us to see everything in black and white, yes and no, good and bad, we continue to see the gray. When we as voters are not in their pocket, they understand that the Independent will correct any significant deviations and so tend to lean toward moderation. It's like attending an open-bar cocktail party under the watchful gaze of a policeman.

11. Refuse to defend, excuse and apologize for everything.

The habit of defending an individual or position at all costs regardless of how shameless, absurd or illogical it may be is a trademark symptom of partisan political intoxication. Displaying a willingness to break from that addiction is a very strong sign that you are truly taking recovery seriously. The willingness for partisans to rise to the defense of anything knows no limits. As a matter of fact, just this morning while perusing several weblogs looking for a very good example, I came across one in a thread about Sarah Palin:

Palin left office because the psychopaths on the left had an army of lawyers filing lawsuit after lawsuit in an effort to destroy her.

See that? It's not her fault she quit the governorship— it's the legal teams dispatched by those terrible left-wing psychopaths! In keeping with long-standing partisan tradition, the friend is absolved of all sins while blame is cast upon the foe. This symptomatic inability to see the forest for the trees is a clear indication of the presence of partisan disorder. Someone who was being truly objective and honest would be hard-pressed to make such a statement since it's abundantly clear to any cognizant, objective individual that the likely reason Mrs. Palin left her job was to use her new-found fame and position to her advantage and make as much money as possible.

It was only moments after the censure of Congressman Charlie Rangel that the commentariat had its say—some of them declared the congressman's censure was "politically motivated" and "racist." Hardly surprising—after all, he was only found guilty of financial malfeasance. Joseph Stalin murdered 20 million of his own people and headed a reign of terror that lasted until his death in 1953, and still has no shortage of apologists pining for his absolution and return.

When our politicians can do no wrong in our eyes, they'll do plenty of wrong.

12. Recognize hypocrisy and carry this message to other partisans and practice these principles in all your affairs.

Another vexatious partisan trait centers around the ability to stand vehemently against the actions and positions of one's foes, while at the same time being willfully blind to, or even endorsing, the same policy for one's friends. Bad. When hypocrisy rears its fat, ugly little head it is essential that it is recognized and beaten senseless. What we believe to be important and noble and legal and ethical begs to be applied across the political spectrum, and not just on a case-by-case basis when it's advantageous and suits you. Do not allow yourself to, in the same breath, condemn one man's infidelity while excusing another's. The guilty are guilty and do not deserve a free pass just because you share the same party pin, in the same way that you should not excuse your neighbor for homicide just because he lives on your street.

By remaining blind and ignorant to the peccadilloes of our public servants we enable the bad and the corrupt to carry on, and we allow bad ideas and bad laws to gain traction.

If the enforcement of our standards and laws isn't bipartisan, if it's selective and strategic and dishonest and partisan, then our standards will remain low and our laws will remain ineffective; and the system will never be fixed.

15

Know "It" When You See "It"

"It" being the B.S. of A.

Unfortunately this book is not a self-help book by any stretch of the imagination. If you had been led to believe that this book might alleviate the effects of chronic bullshit, I apologize. If you started off feeling disenchanted about the state of the union, I would venture to guess you're still feeling the same way. It's also possible that you now find yourself even more disenchanted than before, in which case all I can say is yes, I'm definitely no Dr. Phil. I've always pictured myself more as the Johnny Appleseed of whining.

Speaking of: I've never been more despondent over the state of politics in this country in all my life. Granted, that is not technically a tremendous amount of time because I didn't care about politics for half of my life and during the other half it's only grown incrementally. So I'll adjust my original statement and say that in little more than twenty years of giving a crap about politics, I've never been so incredibly put off by them as I am right now. The policies, the politicians, the electorate. I'd like to run around wagging my finger at everything. I'm annoyed, I'm appalled, I'm worried, I'm angry. I'm incredibly disenchanted, as are you.

Most assuredly some of this disenchantment simply comes from being older and more cynical, from having advanced past that rude-awakening stage discussed in the beginning of the book. We're no longer hopelessly naïve. And I'm starting to think that in the Internet age, despondency travels much, much faster. I just spent some time mining the comment section of the left-wing political blog Hullaballoo and I can tell you this: There are a whole bunch of folks for whom Obama's glow has already faded. *Two years!* They are now officially entering the ranks of the incredibly disenchanted. Welcome. And if you're a Republican, stop with the schadenfreude. I see your love affair with New Jersey governor Chris Christie (really—he could eat a baby and you'd be excited) and I can't help but wonder how that will end for you. But I have an idea. See you soon.

So, you have the broken promises and the squandered potential of the politicians we liked, and the cornucopia of politicians we detest for innumerable reasons. Throw in the fact that we're endlessly hoping for common sense to prevail and that common sense never seems to prevail. Common sense prevailing just once would be nice. We could live off that for a while.

Take all of that frustration and disillusionment and throw in the poo-poo economy and palpable sense of "End of Empire" that we're currently living through and I'm surprised we're not all out running in the streets, screaming. Actually, I'm not that surprised because we can't even seem to be coaxed off the sofa unless Courtney Cox tells us to get out and vote.

IS THERE A PILL FOR THIS?

Oh, if only there were some new kind of prescription for political malaise: *Chillaxin. Contenta. Relaxium.* If the Gods of Pharma can give us six-hour erections, why can't they find a way to make people less excitable about politics? Alas, until that time comes we're just going to have to deal with our problems the old-fashioned way: talking to friends.

Feeling alone? Don't. Misery loves company, and in the case of politics it keeps inviting company to come over and hang out. If I took an informal poll of the six people seated around me we'd all be in agreement that we don't like the way things are and where they're going. We're miserable, agreed. Of course, we'd also have six different opinions on how we could fix the problem, likely ranging from dictatorship to anarchy. That's small beans, though, the kind of details that can be hashed out later. But for now—we really just want to be less miserable. Maybe just a shot of confidence that everything's not going to hell in a handbasket, and the reassurance that the people running the show aren't complete imbeciles. So far they seem to be failing.

We can start by accepting that no system of government is going to be perfect (very smart people have said so!) and that we are bound to experience disagreement and disappointment in varying degrees for a variety of reasons. Taxes will never be low enough or high enough for some of us. We will never be interventionist or isolationist enough to suit some of us. Entitlements will always be too big or too small for some of us. That's the nature of government—please as many of the people as it takes to not get fired. It's imperfect at best. The only people who totally insist that their government is flawless and awesome happen to live in the People's Republic of North

Korea. And that is their strong opinion because the alternative—
your entire family being hauled off to a labor camp—is unappeal-
ing. So, our government is not flawless and awesome by any means
but it does not currently require that we have a photograph of the
Dear Leader prominently displayed in our home. Oh, and we have
food and Internet access. Win some, lose some.

WHAT DO WE DO NOW?

Resolved as we are to make things better, we can endeavor to tone
down our partisan rhetoric and all the mean-spirited us-versus-them
posturing that pits brother against brother, netizen against netizen,
Media Matters against Breitbart, and threatens to tear us apart from
the inside. We should be able to respectfully and intelligently disagree with our peers without resorting to the time-honored tradition
of screaming, yelling and giving someone the finger. I hope, anyway.

I'm incredibly disenchanted but I have not given up. I intend to
be as objective and optimistic as possible in these tough times. This
does not come easy: My default setting is skepticism and cynicism
on almost all issues, from astrology to the assumption that things
always "work out" in the end.

For my part, I intend to make sure that no single party can count
on my unwavering support. I am Independent. To earn my vote,
candidates and issues must pass a test of my design and they will
pass or fail that test on those merits alone. Party affiliation earns
absolutely zero bonus points.

And I will hold politicians, their cheerleaders and the pundits
to task for rank acts of hypocrisy, blind partisanship and for selling out the good of the country for the good of their party. I'll call
bullshit on fiscal conservatives who go on spending sprees. When

a Democratic president pushes for enhanced domestic spying, I'll make sure to remind him how outraged he would have been if a Republican tried the same thing. And when a newly elected congressman who campaigned against ObamaCare gets all hot and bothered that his government insurance isn't kicking in fast enough, I'm happy to join the chorus of folks calling bullshit on Congressman Andy Harris.

Votes will need to be earned. Republicans and Democrats have, for far too long, been able to rely on the *lesser of two evils* vote—secure in the knowledge that at the end of the day, no matter what craptastic candidate they're offering up, a Democrat will vote for the Democratic one and a Republican the Republican one. That cynical reasoning has allowed them to time and again offer up substandard and fringe candidates. By refraining to vote for a *lesser* choice we deny them that power and force them to consider the character, integrity and quality of the candidates they ultimately present to us. If parties continue to offer candidates not worthy of my vote then I will continue to not vote for them, period.

Will bullshit cease to be? Ha! Not in our lifetime. Not as long as there is money to be made peddling it, power to be had by practicing it and plenty of people willing to consume it. But if we can detect it when it presents itself and work hard to prevent contributing to it, we can certainly help see to it that this climate of disenchantment doesn't overpower us and lead to abject misery.

That is what I believe, and will continue to believe until such time as I write a book titled *Quick, Let's Get the Hell out of Here.*

GLOSSARY
Useful political terminology

ACADEMIC

An epithet used by the right to denote someone who by virtue of being in the field of higher education is a *Marxist*.

ACLU

An organization of unflappable lobbyists and lawyers whose strict adherence to core constitutional principles is bound to infuriate you at some point.

ACT

A law that started as a bill but unfortunately no one was able to stop.

AD HOMINEM

An attack that focuses on a politician's lousy character as opposed to his lousy policies.

ADMINISTRATION

The political apparatus composed of the individuals who are making everyone unhappy at that particular moment.

AGENDA

A goal the other guy has that is probably secret and always assumed to be insidious or unacceptable.

AMENDMENT

An addition to the United States Constitution that can be frequently cited by people who don't exactly know what it means.

APOLOGY

A heartfelt way of expressing regret without necessarily admitting guilt.

APPROPRIATIONS

The fancier name for the act of taking taxpayer money and throwing it up in the air.

BALLOT INITIATIVE

A proposed law most voters were unaware of until they stepped into the voting booth.

BIAS

The failure of a member of the *MSM* to agree wholeheartedly with your political position.

BILL
A proposed law printed on a small forest and presented to congressional lawmakers for debate, modification and adding of *riders* to it.

BIPARTISANISM
The belief that you can convince people to abandon their political convictions in favor of yours.

BLUE DOG
A member of the Democratic Party who is hated by the Democratic Party.

BRIEFING
An informational session that often lacks information.

BUDGET
A large book, poorly written and very hard to follow. Though its authors claim it's nonfiction it inevitably gets filed under fantasy.

CAMPAIGN FINANCE REFORM
The process of making contributors seek alternative methods for continuing to give money to their political party of choice.

CAPITALISM
A political system where industry is controlled by private, for-profit entities rather than the state, until they screw it all up and the state steps in.

CENTRIST
An individual who is isn't sure of the political affiliation of the person he's talking to.

CHECKS AND BALANCES

A system that ensures that power is not concentrated in the hands of individuals or groups by not allowing anything to happen.

CHURCH

A popular backdrop for photo opportunities used by candidates for political office.

CLOSED SESSION

A session of Congress that is not open to the public because they don't want you to know what they're talking about because you'd be mad.

CLOTURE

Like a bartender's "last call" but instead of a bunch of drunks it's a bunch of senators and instead of telling them to hurry up and get more booze, he's telling them to shut up and vote on the matter at hand.

COMMUNIST

An individual who yearns for the collective utopias enjoyed by the Soviet Union, China, Vietnam and Cuba, but without all the death and misery. Often believed to be the same as *socialist* by people who don't read books.

CONCESSION

A postelection speech given by the losing candidate that allows him or her to eloquently say *I can't believe that bastard won.*

CONFIRMATION HEARING

A hearing held for the purposes of grandstanding and asking questions that don't get answered.

CONGRESS

The legislative body of the United States, comprising the Senate and the House of Representatives. Vulnerable to ICBMs and located at GPS coordinates N271 W181.

CONGRESSIONAL RECORD

Like C-SPAN, but on paper so it requires more effort to absorb.

CONSERVATIVE

A person who believes you probably shouldn't be doing that.

CONSTITUENT

An individual whose importance is measured by proximity to Election Day.

CONSTITUTION

The document that established the framework of the United States. Largely misunderstood and referred to only when it's advantageous.

DEBATE

A gathering of political candidates for the purpose of explaining their positions by not answering the questions being asked.

DEFICIT

An excess of expenditure that someone else is going to pay for.

DIFFICULT TIME

Excuse often cited as a reason to request that the media stop asking about a mistress.

DISCRETIONARY SPENDING

Money that is wasted with the knowledge that it didn't have to be wasted.

DISTRICT

The geographic area that a representative is responsible for, of no rational shape or size as it is determined largely by gerrymandering.

ELDERLY

A block of voters that becomes valuable during tight races.

ELECTORAL COLLEGE

A body of electors whose purpose and function is not fully understood by people who went to college.

ELITES

A catch-all term for anyone presumed to be smarter.

EMERGENCY SPENDING

An unforeseen expenditure, or a foreseen expenditure masquerading as unforeseen.

ENTITLEMENTS

Government expenditures that are often outrageous and unaffordable unless you directly benefit from them.

EXECUTIVE ORDER

A presidential document that often seeks to create a law instantly, without the trouble of having Congress do it.

EXIT POLL

A reliable way to inaccurately predict how individuals voted.

EXPENDITURE

As in your checkbook, an item that would go under the "debit" column, but with many more digits than your checkbook would allow.

FAIRNESS DOCTRINE

An effort to "level the playing field" in talk radio by making it unpleasant to listen to.

FILIBUSTER

A politician's tactic for delaying debate on a bill by saying even more worthless things than usual.

527 GROUP

A group that avoids legislation against influencing federal elections by influencing federal elections in a different way than lawmakers had imagined they could.

FRANCE

A land in Republican mythology filled with cowards, adulterers and *socialists*.

FREE MARKET

A system where private businesses compete in an unrestricted market, resulting in lower prices for the consumer. Except in pharmaceuticals.

FREEDOM

One of America's chief exports, often delivered with force in rare instances where it isn't really wanted.

GERRYMANDER

The accidental creation of abstract art by the intentional creation of districts that favor one political direction.

GOD

An unseen force that always appears at the end of political speeches.

GOP

Acronym for "Grand Old Party," which once popularly referred to the Republican Party, which is now known as "Those bastards."

HARD MONEY

Money that comes from your personal banking account and therefore is "hard" to part with.

HERO

Initially used to refer to an individual who selflessly gave their life while in service to others. Now used to refer to anyone who has died.

HITLER

An incredibly evil historical figure responsible for the death of millions and often equated with a person who says/does something you're not fond of.

IMPEACHMENT

To charge the holder of an office with misconduct, especially if he or she is in an opposing political party.

INDEPENDENT

A very untrustworthy person who can't decide if they're Republican or Democrat.

INTERN

Fair game.

IOWA

A state that doubles in population briefly every presidential election.

JOINT COMMITTEE

A committee comprised of both Senate and House members, or "the big guys" and "the little guys."

JOINT RESOLUTION

A measure that requires approval of both the House and the Senate. Once required to declare war, as opposed to the current "At the president's whim" policy.

LAME DUCK

A politician who, because of term limits or because he didn't get reelected, will be a lobbyist or consultant soon.

LIBERAL

A person who is willing to eschew many traditional values and watch Brazilian tranny porn.

LOBBYIST

A person who pushes for legislation beneficial to the people signing her paycheck.

LOG CABIN REPUBLICANS

The world's most forgiving homosexuals.

MAJORITY LEADER

The most hated person in the majority party.

MAJORITY PARTY

The party currently tasked with driving the country off a cliff.

MARXIST

A *communist* who reads books and has prescription lenses.

MINORITY LEADER

Unfortunately, Al Sharpton.

MISSPEAK

An acknowledgment that one has lied, without admitting such.

MODERATE

A member of the opposition, admired by your party and hated by his own.

MSM

Acronym for "Mainstream media," which is believed to suffer from *bias.*

NAZI

A member of the National Socialist German Worker's Party who often used brutal means to support racist and authoritarian views, or someone you don't like because of his position on farm subsidies.

NEOCON

Used as a derogatory term to identify an adherent of a right-wing political philosophy that few people actually understand.

OMNIBUS BILL

A bill stuffed with all sorts of related and unrelated stuff, just like the omnibus drawer in your kitchen.

PLATFORM

The declared position of a particular political party, as opposed to its true shadowy agenda.

POCKET VETO

A passive-aggressive way for a president to allow a bill to die by allowing the legislative session to expire before signing it.

POLITICS

The art of telling everyone else what they're going to do and how they're going to do it.

POLLSTER

An individual who attempts to confirm your gut feeling.

PORK

Spending authorizations for projects, like a blimp factory, tacked on to bills that have absolutely nothing to do with blimp factories.

PRESIDENT

The head of the United States government, chosen by election or the Supreme Court.

PRIMARY RACE

Competition for a party nomination that involves declaring colleagues unfit to govern unless they manage to clinch the nomination.

PROGRESSIVE TAX

A tax rate that increases as an individual's income increases, which is acceptable unless you're that individual.

PUNDIT

A person who, by virtue of being on television, is an expert on all things.

RANKING MEMBER

The most entrenched member in the room.

READING

That which often does not occur prior to passage of a bill.

RECESS

A treasured time when kids and politicians run around and don't do anything.

RECOUNT

A retally of votes considered a necessity if your candidate requests one, sore sportsmanship if the other candidate does.

REVENUE ENHANCEMENT

A tax increase—sugarcoated in the same doublespeak as Ticketmaster's "convenience fee."

RIDER

Something tacked on to a bill, often at the last minute, often with the politician pointing to the horizon and saying, "Look over there!"

RINO

For "Republican In Name Only," a freethinking member of the Republican Party who is hated for his steadfast adherence to principle.

ROLL

The complete list of the members of House and Senate, several of whom will likely be robocalling you in the near future.

SENIORITY

Proof that life is no different than high school.

SOCIALIST

An eighteen-year-old attending a liberal arts college. Also used to identify someone as an enemy of capitalism and America. Often equated with *communist* by people whose opinions are formed by sound bites.

SOFT MONEY

Money that is not hard and is therefore able to squeeze past the various obstacles put in place to prevent it from going where it's going.

SPIN

The ability to point to a tomato and say, "That is not a tomato. It is a houseboat."

SPONSOR

A congressman who has attached his or her name to a bill, so that he or she may be remembered/cursed by name fifty years in the future.

SUPPLEMENTAL

A nice way of saying "budgets don't matter."

SURPLUS

The opposite of a deficit. You will never see this word again.

SWING VOTER

An individual whose inability to be strictly partisan is extremely disturbing to campaign managers.

TABLING

Putting a bill aside for later consideration. The equivalent of saying, "I'll call you," while knowing you won't.

TALKING POINTS

Sentiment that, without regard to context, must be repeated until the interview has concluded.

UNFUNDED MANDATE

Sending Billy to the store for a pack of cigarettes but not giving Billy any money for them.

UNION

An assembly of empowered workers, or a gathering of communists.

VETO

FDR's favorite pastime.

VOTER

A person with little or no background in politics entrusted with hiring or firing politicians.

WATCHDOG

An organization engaged in making mountains out of molehills on a daily basis.

WHIP

Like a Catholic nun, but in Congress.

WIFE

The woman standing beside the man telling reporters about his three-year affair with a cocktail waitress.

WONK

A nerd that eschews Dungeons & Dragons in favor of politics.

ACKNOWLEDGMENTS

I thank: My lovely agent, Sara Crowe at Harvey Klinger, who got the book into the right hands, which turned out to be those of Mitchell Ivers at Threshold Editions. The first time I actually spoke with Mitch was over the phone when I was on morphine (not recreationally—I'd had a spinal tap). I don't remember our first conversation much, but before succumbing to morphine's sweet, sweet embrace I mumbled something about the "climate of incredible disenchantment." He liked the sound of that and later suggested that I tweak the original subtitle. So the revised subtitle comes to you courtesy of a Schedule II narcotic. A wonderful, wonderful Schedule II narcotic to which I would most certainly become addicted if it were at all practical.

Every writer is, I've noticed, neurotic in some capacity. They always seem to have a specific way of going about writing. Some people need music, a special chair, a perfectly positioned desk, constant smoke breaks, gum, white noise, alcohol. I need silence and to be as far from the Internet as possible.

Fortunately I married a very no-drama, low-maintenance, high-IQ woman who understands my neuroses and is willing to accommodate these artistic/creative/annoying needs. While writing this I spent a great deal of time away from her and the children I very much adore and she picked up all of that parental slack. She did so without complaint, I might add. Instead, she merely said, "You owe me," every time I came back. I married a great woman. This is something her ex-boyfriends seem to have realized, because they keep reaching out to her on Facebook. So, thank you, darling Ewa, and please ignore those bastards on Facebook.

This book was written on a MacBook Pro that I dropped on a hard floor not long after purchasing it. It has a dent and makes an occasional alarming noise, but you can apparently still write a book on it. For that I used the fantastic writing program Scrivener, which was recommended to me by another author, Seth Mnookin, who is always quick with a lozenge when I cough. Not because he cares about my cough, mind you, but because it annoys the hell out of him.

I did a lot of work on the book at Paragraph, a New York City writer's studio located above an Asian massage parlor. Paragraph is run by Joy Parisi and Lila Cecil, two lovely ladies who have the amazing ability to tolerate droves of unbalanced screenwriters, journalists, poets and authors.

During the writing process I drank ridiculous amounts of coffee (Starbucks) and tea (Stash), didn't shave (Mach 3), ate crap for lunch (Bit-O-Honey) and in the long stretches alone in the country, absent human contact, tended to take a pass on deodorant (Degree) and oral hygiene (Tom's of Maine).